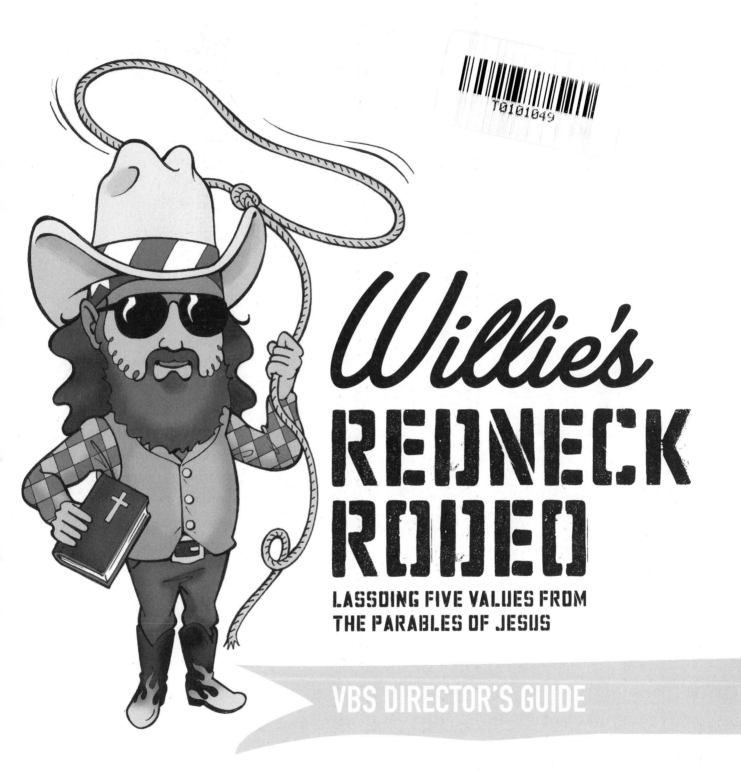

Willie's REDNECK RODEO

LASSOING FIVE VALUES FROM THE PARABLES OF JESUS

VBS DIRECTOR'S GUIDE

KORIE ROBERTSON & CHRYS HOWARD

ZONDERVAN®

ZONDERVAN

Willie's Redneck Rodeo VBS Director's Guide
Copyright © 2014 by Korie Robertson and Chrys Howard

Requests for information should be addressed to:

Zondervan, 3900 *Sparks Dr. SE, Grand Rapids, MI 49546*

ISBN 978-0-310-88452-1

Photos of characters are © Russell A. Graves unless otherwise noted.

Cover design: Grey Matter Group
Cover illustration: Michael Hunt
Interior design: David Conn

Printed in the United States of America

14 15 16 17 18 19 20 21 22 23 / 20 19 18 17 16 15 14 13 12 11 10 9 8 7 6 5 4 3 2 1

CONTENTS

SECTION FOUR: RODEO STATIONS

SECTION FIVE: RODEO RESOURCES

ACKNOWLEDGMENTS

We would like to thank our friend and children's minister, LinDee Loveland, for her incredible contribution to *Willie's Redneck Rodeo*. She is a bottomless pit of great ideas and blesses our lives every day. Our children love Miss LinDee and we do too!

We would also like to thank Karen Lee-Thorp and Cindy Bultema. What a blessing to have such talented women help us on the *Faith Commander* adult and teen books (Karen), and children's curriculum (Cindy). They caught the vision and ran with it. You both are amazing!

A special thank you to the video crew, T. J. Rathbun, Jay Irwin, and John Pottenger, who came to Louisiana to capture who the Robertsons really are.

And to Alan, Jase, Willie, Jep, Si, Phil, Reed, John Luke, Sadie, Cole, and Will who took time out of their busy lives to lend a voice to this project. You guys are awesome men of God, and Sadie, you're an awesome God-girl!

Thank you, John Raymond, for your faith in this project and for your desire to "get it right" for the sake of the adults and children who we pray will be blessed by it. You and your entire team have been amazing to work with. We couldn't have asked for a better experience.

WELCOME TO WILLIE'S REDNECK RODEO!

If you're a fan of Willie, Korie, and the whole Robertson gang, we want to thank you for watching the *Duck Dynasty*® TV show. It's fun to share our lives with you, and we hope that we are able to entertain you with our silly actions. Most importantly, we want to influence those who watch the show with a Christlike example.

Today's world is full of activities that are opposite of what is pleasing to God. Children need the truth of God's Word in their lives, and in this VBS our goal is to help them gain a better understanding of the parables of Jesus and how those parables should guide their behavior. Jesus was a powerful storyteller, and in this VBS we will provide some modern-day retellings of those parables so that your kids will see that God's laws are just as important today as they were two thousand years ago.

We chose the title *Willie's Redneck Rodeo* because rodeos are a big part of the southern culture where we live. Rodeos are challenging for those who participate in them, but they are also lots of fun. Every rodeo has cowboys falling off bulls, young kids roping calves, teenagers riding horses around barrels, and clowns keeping everyone laughing. It's kind of like working at Duck Commander®!

Life is like that as well. Some days are fun, some are crazy, some are exciting, and some are challenging. Life is a journey. But if we learn to "lasso" the teachings of Jesus, each day will have more meaning for us as we head toward our ultimate goal of spending eternity in heaven with Christ.

We hope that you and your church family have a lot of fun with Willie and the gang. But most importantly, we pray that your children will experience the love of God, learn from God's Word, and be strengthened in their faith.

In Him,
Korie and Chrys

1

ABOUT THE RODEO

GENERAL OVERVIEW

Willie's Redneck Rodeo is a Vacation Bible School program that will help you reach children ages four through twelve with the gospel of Jesus Christ. Each day, the children will learn about a parable that Jesus taught in the Gospels as told through the cast of the *Duck Dynasty*® television show. The children will begin at an opening Roundup, where characters portraying the Robertsons will introduce the following themes.

- **Day One–Redonkulous Faith:** During this opening session, the children will learn that having a *redonkulous faith* means to have a ridiculous amount of faith. Sometimes this faith might be as little as a mustard seed, but it can prove to be as powerful as a mighty wind! The children will also discover that believing in God means having faith in Him and trusting that He is their defender, deliverer, and provider. This faith will grow as they witness God doing things in their lives, and it will carry them through the times when they wonder if what they are facing is too large for even God to handle.

- **Day Two–Radical Forgiveness:** During this second session, the children will learn that *radical forgiveness* means to forgive in such a way that others might not understand it—such as when someone hurts them or embarrasses them, but they choose to forgive that person anyway. God calls all of His children to forgive just as He has forgiven them—even when it is difficult—and this lesson will stress this important point. The kids will also learn that forgiving is different than *forgetting*, for they might still remember the offense even though they choose to forgive the person who committed it.

- **Day Three–Ravenous Prayer:** During this third session, the children will learn that having a *ravenous prayer* life means to have an unquenchable thirst for talking to God and for listening to Him. They will discover that the Bible tells them to pray continually, which means to always have a heart that is open to God's Word and a mouth that is always willing to ask God to supply their needs. They will discover that they can call on God to give them wisdom, strength, comfort, or anything else they need. God is good all the time and is always ready to listen and supply what His children need!

- **Day Four–Real Obedience:** During this fourth session, the children will learn that *real obedience* comes from the heart. It means listening to their parents and obeying them the first time they are asked to do something—not the third or fifth time they have been asked. The kids will learn that the Bible says we are to obey our parents because this is an important way that we learn how to obey our heavenly Father. Life is so much easier when we learn to obey!

- **Day Five—Rowdy Kindness:** During this final session, the children will learn that *rowdy kindness* means to be LOUD about being kind! Being rowdy about kindness means choosing to treat everyone with a kind and respectful spirit and looking at them the way that God does. It means looking past a person's faults and focusing on his or her needs rather than their own. The kids will learn that God has asked them to treat others with kindness, and nothing should get in the way of them keeping that command.

The children will explore each of these themes by attending various stations each day, including Missy's Music and Memory (singing and memory work), Korie's Craft Shed (arts and crafts), the Warehouse (games), Miss Kay's Kitchen (snacks and lessons), and Si's Bull Pen (fun facts and activities). A final Closing Roundup will sum up the theme and close out the day's events.

THE CAST

Just in case you're not familiar with the Robertson family from *Duck Dynasty*®, we thought we would tell you who's who before we begin. Here are all the family members your kids will be getting to know during their time at Willie's Redneck Rodeo.

PHIL ROBERTSON
Dad
Skit actor

WILLIE ROBERTSON
Son of Phil and Kay
Station and skit actor

"UNCLE" SI ROBERTSON
Brother of Phil
Station and skit actor

MISS KAY
Mom
Station and skit actor

© Steven Palowsky

KORIE ROBERTSON
Wife of Willie
Station and skit actor

JASE ROBERTSON
Son of Phil and Kay
Skit actor

MISSY ROBERTSON
Wife of Jase
Station actor

JOHN LUKE ROBERTSON
Son of Willie and Korie
Skit actor

GODWIN
Duck Commander team member
Skit actor

JEP ROBERTSON
Son of Phil and Kay
Skit actor

SADIE ROBERTSON
Daughter of Willie and Korie
Skit actor

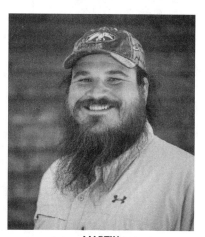

MARTIN
Duck Commander team member
Skit actor

BELLA ROBERTSON
Daughter of Willie and Korie
Skit actor

WILL ROBERTSON
Son of Willie and Korie
Skit actor

MOUNTAIN MAN
Robertsons' neighbor
Skit actor

BIRD'S-EYE VIEW OF THE RODEO

	DAY 1	DAY 2	DAY 3	DAY 4	DAY 5
The Theme	Redonkulous Faith	Radical Forgiveness	Ravenous Prayer	Real Obedience	Rowdy Kindness
The Point	Following God requires a "redonkulous" amount of faith!	It is important to forgive others as God has forgiven us.	God listens to the prayers of His children and delights in providing for their needs.	God calls us to obey Him and others in authority over us.	God is kind toward us, so we should also treat others in a kind way.
Memory Verse	1 Corinthians 16:13	Colossians 3:13	Philippians 4:6	2 John 1:6	Colossians 3:12
Preschool and Elementary	"Be on your guard. Stand firm in the faith."	"Forgive, just as the Lord forgave you."	"Tell God about everything. Ask and pray. Give thanks to him."	"The way we show our love is to obey God's commands."	"Put on tender mercy and kindness as if they were your clothes."
Later Elementary	"Be on your guard. Stand firm in the faith. Be brave. Be strong."	"Put up with each other. Forgive the things you are holding against one another. Forgive, just as the Lord forgave you."	"Don't worry about anything. Instead, tell God about everything. Ask and pray. Give thanks to him."	"The way we show our love is to obey God's commands. He commands you to lead a life of love."	"You are God's chosen people. You are holy and dearly loved. So put on tender mercy and kindness as if they were your clothes. Don't be proud. Be gentle and patient."
Bible Story	Parable of the Sower (Matthew 13:1–23)	Parable of the Unmerciful Servant (Matthew 18:21–35)	Parable of the Friend in Need (Luke 11:5–10)	Parable of the Two Sons (Matthew 21:28–32)	Parable of the Good Samaritan (Luke 10:25–37)

DETAILED SUMMARY OF THE RODEO

	THEME AND MEMORY VERSE	OPENING ROUNDUP	MISSY'S MUSIC AND MEMORY
DAY 1	**Redonkulous Faith** **Memory Verse:** 1 Corinthians 16:13 **Preschool and Early Elementary:** "Be on your guard. Stand firm in the faith." **Later Elementary:** "Be on your guard. Stand firm in the faith. Be brave. Be strong."	**Bible Story:** The Parable of the Sower (Matthew 13:1–23) **Main Idea:** Following God requires a "redonkulous" amount of faith!	**Music:** 1. "By Faith" (Jeff Slaughter) 2. "Faith" (*Sing 'Em Again: Favorite VBS Songs for Families*, vol. 3) 3. "We Can Trust Him" (*Sing 'Em Again: Favorite VBS Songs for Families*, vol. 5) 4. "King of the Jungle" (*Great Worship Songs for Kids*, vol. 1) 5. "The One True God" (*Sing 'Em Again; Favorite Holy Land VBS Songs for Families*, vol. 2) **Memory Game:** Pass the Ball
DAY 2	**Radical Forgiveness** **Memory Verse:** Colossians 3:13 **Preschool and Early Elementary:** "Forgive, just as the Lord forgave you." **Later Elementary:** "Put up with each other. Forgive the things you are holding against one another. Forgive, just as the Lord forgave you."	**Bible Story:** The Parable of the Unmerciful Servant (Matthew 18:21–35) **Main Idea:** God wants us to forgive others in a radical way!	**Music:** 1. "His Great Love" (*Pandamania* VBS) 2. "Revelation Song" (*Great Worship Songs for Kids*, vol. 5) 3. "East to West" (Casting Crowns) 4. "Do to Others" (*God's Word in My Heart: Scripture Songs for Families*) 5. "Give as Freely" (*God's Word in My Heart: Scripture Songs for Families*) **Memory Game:** God's Treasure
DAY 3	**Ravenous Prayer** **Memory Verse:** Philippians 4:6 **Preschool and Early Elementary:** "Tell God about everything. Ask and pray. Give thanks to him." **Later Elementary:** "Don't worry about anything. Instead, tell God about everything. Ask and pray. Give thanks to him."	**Bible Story:** The Parable of the Friend in Need (Luke 11:5–10) **Main Idea:** God tells us in the Bible that we are to be persistent—or "ravenous"—in prayer!	**Music:** 1. "Watching Over You" (*Favorite VBS Songs for Families*) 2. "Great Big God" (*Great Big God*) 3. "Rejoice in the Lord Always" (*God's Word in My Heart: Scripture Songs for Families*) 4. "Ask (and It Will Be Given)" (*More Sing-a-Long Scripture Songs*) 5. "Keep On" (*God's Word in My Heart: Scripture Songs for Families*) 6. "Love and Pray" (*God's Word in My Heart: Scripture Songs for Families*) **Memory Game:** King of the Mountain
DAY 4	**Real Obedience** **Memory Verse:** 2 John 1:6 **Preschool and Early Elementary:** "The way we show our love is to obey God's commands." **Later Elementary:** "The way we show our love is to obey God's commands. He commands you to lead a life of love."	**Bible Story:** The Parable of the Two Sons (Matthew 21:28–32) **Main Idea:** It takes real obedience for us to obey God and follow His commands!	**Music:** 1. "You, You, You" (Sky VBS) 2. "I Believe in Jesus" (*Super Strong God*) 3. "Obey My Commandments" (*God's Word in My Heart: Scripture Songs for Families*) 4. "The Lord's Plans" (*Sing 'Em Again: Favorite Holy Land VBS Songs for Families*, vol. 2) 5. "Trust in the Lord" (*More Sing-a-Long Scripture Songs*) **Memory Game:** Concentrate!
DAY 5	**Rowdy Kindness** **Memory Verse:** Colossians 3:12 **Preschool and Early Elementary:** "Put on tender mercy and kindness as if they were your clothes." **Later Elementary:** "You are God's chosen people. You are holy and dearly loved. So put on tender mercy and kindness as if they were your clothes. Don't be proud. Be gentle and patient."	**Bible Story:** The Parable of the Good Samaritan (Luke 10:25–37) **Main Idea:** God wants us to be loud and rowdy when it comes to being kind to others!	**Music:** 1. "Live It Out" (*Big Apple Adventure VBS*) 2. "Every Move I Make" (*Great Worship Songs for Kids*, vol. 1) 3. "How Can I Keep from Singing" (*Great Worship Songs for Kids*, vol. 2) 4. "Hands and Feet" (*Great Worship Songs for Kids*, vol. 2) 5. "Let Your Light Shine" (*God's Word in My Heart: Scripture Songs for Families*) **Memory Game:** Memory Puzzle

KORIE'S CRAFT SHED	THE WAREHOUSE	MISS KAY'S KITCHEN	UNCLE SI'S BULL PEN
Craft: Coffee Filter Flowers **Main Idea:** Our faith grows as we study God's Word and look at His creation.	**Game #1 (All Ages):** Barrel Races **Game #2 (All Ages):** Willie's Bowling Alley **Game #3 (All Ages):** Who's the Tallest **Main Idea:** Teamwork requires putting your faith in another person, just as trusting God requires you to put your faith in Him.	**Snack:** Heart Cookies **Main Idea:** Following God requires a "redonkulous" amount of faith!	**Activity for Older Children:** Understanding Faith **Activity for Younger Children:** Faith in God's Creation
Craft: Unmerciful Servant Puppets **Main Idea:** God wants us to forgive others no matter who they are or what they have done.	**Game #1 (All Ages):** Ducks and Decoys **Game #2 (Older Children):** Duck Hunt Dodge Ball **Game #3 (Younger Children):** Ducks Flying Over and Under **Main Idea:** As the Parable of the Unmerciful Servant shows, we must always choose to forgive those who have wronged us.	**Snack:** Silver Coins (Ritz Crackers) **Main Idea:** God wants us to forgive others in a radical way!	**Activity for Older Children:** Forgiveness Acronym **Activity for Younger Children:** Forgiveness Activity Sheet
Craft: Prayer Journals **Main Idea:** God wants us to keep asking, seeking, and knocking on heaven's door when we go to Him in prayer.	**Game #1 (All Ages):** Steal the Decoy **Game #2 (All Ages):** Animal Connection **Game #3 (All Ages):** Sit Down If … **Main Idea:** God is available to talk with us at any time, and He wants to hear from us. We just have to figure out how to not let distractions get in our way.	**Snack:** Power Snack (Trail Mix) **Main Idea:** God listens to our prayers and delights in providing for our needs.	**Activity for Older Children:** Prayer That Pleases God **Activity for Younger Children:** Ravenous Prayer Activity Sheet
Craft: Paper Plate Art **Main Idea:** Obeying our parents pleases God and is a great way to honor Him.	**Game #1 (All Ages):** Just Like the Robertsons **Game #2 (Older Children):** Blind Obedience Obstacle Course **Game #3 (Younger Children):** Miss Kay's in the Kitchen **Main Idea:** God doesn't ask us to obey Him because He likes to see us move around obstacles. Instead, He gives us instructions for our own good.	**Snack:** Dirt Dessert (Chocolate Pudding and Gummy Worms) **Main Idea:** Sometimes it might seem like no fun when God asks us to obey, but we have to remember that it is for our own benefit and our own good.	**Activity for Older Children:** Obedience Scripture Search **Activity for Younger Children:** Obedience Activity Sheet
Craft: Kindness Mural **Main Idea:** There are many little ways that we can show kindness to others each day!	**Game #1 (All Ages):** Blind Hunting Dog **Game #2 (Older Children):** Camo Relay Race **Game #3 (Younger Children):** Duck, Duck, Hunter **Main Idea:** There are always people in our lives to whom we can show kindness. When we do, it not only helps the other person, but it can help us as well!	**Snack:** Special Teddies (Teddy Grahams) **Main Idea:** God wants us to be loud and rowdy when it comes to being kind to others!	**Activity for Older Children:** Kindness Makes a Difference **Activity for Younger Children:** Kindness Activity Sheet

PLANNING THE RODEO

PLANNING TIMELINE

As the director of Willie's Redneck Rodeo, you are in charge of the whole show. That's no small job! So let's get started with some of the details you will need to put in place to help you pull off the best rodeo your town has ever seen. Note that the following is not an exhaustive list of everything you might need to cover, but it will give you a general sense of what you need to do to get your rodeo off the ground.

TWELVE MONTHS BEFORE

- Set the dates for when you will be holding Willie's Redneck Rodeo at your church. Make sure it is on the church calendar.
- Begin drafting your budget (see "Rodeo Resources" on page 155). Request the budget from your church that you will need.

FOUR TO SIX MONTHS BEFORE

- Decide on the number of children your church can accommodate.
- Begin making a master list of all the supplies you will need to order in advance (see "Master Supply List" on pages 23–24).
- Think through your advertising strategy. How will you get the word out that Willie's Redneck Rodeo is coming to town? (See "Talkin' It Up" on pages 43–44.)
- Think through your student registration. Will it be online, in person, or both? If you are doing online registration, who can help you set that up?

TWO TO THREE MONTHS BEFORE

- Post the dates you will be holding Willie's Redneck Rodeo on your church's website.
- Begin forming your team of leaders and volunteers. Do "in-person asks" to each of your key leaders. (See "Gathering Your Volunteers" on pages 29–33.)
- Begin making "save the date" announcements in church.
- Start to enact your advertising plan (in the community, through social media, and whatever other means you have established).
- Order your supplies.
- Open online and in-person student registration.

ONE MONTH BEFORE

- Set the date you will be holding a training workshop for your volunteers and announce it to your church.
- Send out an email to all church attenders with details on student registration. If possible, include an online link (see "Talkin' It Up" on pages 43–44).
- Think through on-site logistics such as check-in/check-out stations, child safety, directional signs, and so forth.
- Begin placing inserts for the upcoming VBS in your church bulletins (see "Bulletin Insert" on page 44).
- Post flyers in your community. Mail flyers to students who attended last year's VBS.

TWO WEEKS BEFORE

- Conduct your volunteer training workshop. This can be done during lunch after church or during a short meeting after the main service. Be sure to get your volunteers revved up about the rodeo! Also, don't forget to prepare the necessary volunteer materials for the meeting, including VBS schedules, job descriptions, rotation station materials, and so forth.
- Begin Facebook and Twitter promotion (see page 43 in "Talkin' It Up").

ONE WEEK TO ONE DAY BEFORE

- Close your student registration.
- Take a deep breath and continue to pray. The rodeo will be great!
- Print student and volunteer nametags.
- Pick up T-shirts (if applicable).
- Set up the rooms for the Opening/Closing Roundup and for each of the stations. Post the names of the stations and create directional signs as needed. (See "The Roundup Experience" on pages 47–49 and the station explanations on pages 99–152 for more details.)
- Prepare volunteer leaders' clipboards with student rosters, registration details, and other information they need to perform their duties for the VBS.
- Print out extra copies of the handouts in this director's guide for any volunteers who did not bring it with them to the first session.

MASTER SUPPLY LIST

The following are a few items that you will need to purchase in order to make the VBS the best experience possible for your children. Once again, this is not an exhaustive list of everything you might need, but it will help you get the show on the road.

FOR VOLUNTEERS

- Volunteer appreciation gift (optional)
- T-shirts with *Willie's Redneck Rodeo* logo (optional—see the DVD-ROM for a JPEG of the logo)

RODEO REGISTRATION/ CHECK-IN DESK

- Rodeo registration forms and check-in/ check-out sheet (see pages 156–159)
- Nametags for kids and volunteers (optional)
- T-shirts or any giveaway items that students receive with registration (optional)
- Cash box (for checks and cash)

OPENING AND CLOSING ROUNDUPS

- Costumes for actors (see scripts on pages 51–96 for outfits needed each day)
- Sound and video equipment
- Set and background props (see pages 47–48)
- A whistle (for some of the skits and to dismiss the kids to their stations)
- Additional props (see pages 51–96)

MISSY'S MUSIC AND MEMORY

- Sound and video equipment
- Music CDs, MP4s, or Rockin' Rednecks live band
- Pictures of Missy (full color or gray scale—see DVD-ROM)
- Large foam squares that lock together or rugs (optional)
- Memory activities (see pages 99–106 for activities needed each day)

KORIE'S CRAFT SHED

- A picture of Korie to post in the room (full color or gray scale—see DVD-ROM)
- Plastic tablecloths and masking tape (optional)
- Large plastic tarps (optional)
- Shed-like props such as flowerpots, hammers, shovels, or pieces of wood
- Craft supplies (see pages 107–111 for supplies needed each day)

THE WAREHOUSE

- A whistle (for getting the children's attention)
- Pictures of Jase, Willie, Jep, and/or Si (full color or gray scale—see DVD-ROM)
- A sign that says "Duck Commander"
- Costumes for your station actors (see Opening Roundup skits) and nametags (optional)
- Duck Commander T-shirts for your other volunteers (optional)
- Game equipment (see pages 114–121 for equipment needed each day)

MISS KAY'S KITCHEN

- Picture of Miss Kay (full color or gray scale—see DVD-ROM)
- Pictures of the Robertson boys or other duck-related items (optional)
- Kitchen-like props such as utensils, pans, or jars of spices
- Plastic tablecloths and masking tape (optional)
- Large plastic tarps (optional)
- Costume for Miss Kay (see Opening Roundup skits)
- Snack/recipe items (see pages 123–134)

SI'S BULL PEN

- Picture of Si and/or other Robertsons (full color or gray scale—see DVD-ROM)
- Costume for Si (see Opening Roundup skits)
- Pencils and crayons
- Bibles
- Si fact sheets and reproducible activity sheets (see pages 135–152)

ROTATION SCHEDULES

As mentioned in the Planning Timeline, one of the first things you need to consider when putting together your VBS program is how many students your church or facility can accommodate. From there, you need to think about how many days you want your rodeo to last, what schedule would work best for your kids and volunteers, and whether you want to do a morning or evening program. On the following pages, you will find three sample schedules that you can use to customize your VBS experience. Of course, as always, feel free to come up with your own schedule that works best for you.

A NOTE ABOUT AGES AND STAGES

If your church is like many today, you will want to customize your VBS stations for different age groups. Generally, it works well to divide students into three groups: (1) preschoolers (four- and five-year-olds), (2) early elementary (kindergarten through second grade), and (3) later elementary (third through fifth grade). Using same-age groups such as these will offer you the following benefits:

- Newcomers may already know some of the children in their groups from class at school.
- The children may feel more comfortable being with others of their same age and more willing to participate in the activities.
- Grouping kids by age is simple and makes it easier to make last-minute registration changes on the first day.
- The station leaders can more easily adapt the lessons to meet the specific skills sets of the group.

Dividing the children by age can be especially beneficial for Missy's Music and Memory station, the Warehouse, and Si's Bull Pen. For this reason, specific options for older and younger children have been included in those station descriptions. In addition, you may need to customize some of the options for Korie's Craft Shed and Miss Kay's Kitchen to better fit the ages of your registered rodeo participants.

If your VBS will be smaller in size, you might want to instead opt for mixed-age groups. In such cases, you might end up with a group that has three first-graders, a second-grader, and two fourth-graders. While the arrangement may add some complexities to your VBS, it can also offer the following benefits:

- The older children may develop a supportive relationship with the younger kids in the group. This can actually help to keep both age groups on track.
- The older and more mature kids in the groups may actually serve as assistant leaders, helping to keep the rest of the children on track. This can help greatly with discipline problems.
- The older kids may enjoy having younger kids look up to them.
- Mixed-age groups allow the children to form friendships with others that they might not have otherwise befriended.

In the end, the choice is yours for how you want to arrange your groups. Just know that both options work and that your VBS will run smoothly regardless of the particular option you choose.

PRINT IT OUT!

Once you've customized your rotation schedule, be sure to print out a copy for all your group volunteers. They will need to follow the times carefully to make sure they move their groups to the right stations at the right times. You can post a rotation schedule in each room and also place small versions of the schedule on lanyards for volunteers to hang around their necks or carry in their pockets. With a simple rotation schedule and good communication, your VBS sessions will move smoothly and efficiently!

CLASSIC SCHEDULE

FIVE-DAY, HALF-DAY SCHEDULE
(Total running time: 3.25 hours per day)

This is the classic or traditional VBS schedule. Each station lasts approximately 25 minutes, with 5 minutes in between stations for the children to get settled. Morning and evening options are provided.

	GROUP 1	GROUP 2	GROUP 3	GROUP 4	GROUP 5
9:00–9:25 am 5:30–5:55 pm	Opening Roundup	Opening Roundup	Opening Roundup	Opening Roundup	Opening Roundup
9:30–9:55 am 6:00–6:25 pm	Missy's Music and Memory	Si's Bull Pen	Miss Kay's Kitchen	The Warehouse	Korie's Craft Shed
10:00–10:25 am 6:30–6:55 pm	Korie's Craft Shed	Missy's Music and Memory	Si's Bull Pen	Miss Kay's Kitchen	The Warehouse
10:30–10:55 am 7:00–7:25 pm	The Warehouse	Korie's Craft Shed	Missy's Music and Memory	Si's Bull Pen	Miss Kay's Kitchen
11:00–11:25 am 7:30–7:55 pm	Miss Kay's Kitchen	The Warehouse	Korie's Craft Shed	Missy's Music and Memory	Si's Bull Pen
11:30–11:55 am 8:00–8:25 pm	Si's Bull Pen	Miss Kay's Kitchen	The Warehouse	Korie's Craft Shed	Missy's Music and Memory
12:00–12:15 pm 8:30–8:45 pm	Closing Roundup	Closing Roundup	Closing Roundup	Closing Roundup	Closing Roundup

SHORTENED SCHEDULE

FIVE-DAY, HALF-DAY SCHEDULE

(Total running time: 2.00 hours per day)

This is an abbreviated version of the classic VBS schedule. Each station lasts approximately 15 minutes, and no time is given in between stations. Morning and evening options are provided.

	GROUP 1	GROUP 2	GROUP 3	GROUP 4	GROUP 5
9:00 – 9:25 am 5:30 – 5:55 pm	Opening Roundup	Opening Roundup	Opening Roundup	Opening Roundup	Opening Roundup
9:30 – 9:45 am 6:00 – 6:15 pm	Missy's Music and Memory	Si's Bull Pen	Miss Kay's Kitchen	The Warehouse	Korie's Craft Shed
9:45 – 10:00 am 6:15 – 6:30 pm	Korie's Craft Shed	Missy's Music and Memory	Si's Bull Pen	Miss Kay's Kitchen	The Warehouse
10:00 – 10:15 am 6:30 – 6:45 pm	The Warehouse	Korie's Craft Shed	Missy's Music and Memory	Si's Bull Pen	Miss Kay's Kitchen
10:15 – 10:30 am 6:45 – 7:00 pm	Miss Kay's Kitchen	The Warehouse	Korie's Craft Shed	Missy's Music and Memory	Si's Bull Pen
10:30 – 10:45 am 7:00 – 7:15 pm	Si's Bull Pen	Miss Kay's Kitchen	The Warehouse	Korie's Craft Shed	Missy's Music and Memory
10:45 – 11:00 am 7:15 – 7:30 pm	Closing Roundup	Closing Roundup	Closing Roundup	Closing Roundup	Closing Roundup

THREE-DAY, ALL-DAY SCHEDULE (WITH LUNCH)

(Total running time: 8 hours, 20 minutes per day)

This version of the scheduled condenses five half-days' worth of VBS material into three full days. Times and themes for each session covered are given below. This schedule includes a "free choice" option on Day 3, where the kids can choose which games or activities to do. Feel free to use any of the recipes from the Miss Kay's Kitchen station for snacks or lunchtime.

	DAY 1	DAY 2	DAY 3
9:00 – 9:25 am	Opening Roundup	Opening Roundup	Opening Roundup
9:30 – 10:30 am	**Korie's Crafts** (Faith): groups 1, 2, and 3 **Warehouse** (Faith): groups 4 and 5	**Korie's Crafts** (Prayer): groups 1, 2, and 3 **Warehouse** (Prayer): groups 4 and 5	**Korie's Crafts** (Kindness): groups 1, 2, and 3 **Warehouse** (Kindness): groups 4 and 5
10:35 – 11:15 am	**Missy's Music** (Faith): all groups	**Missy's Music** (Prayer): all groups	**Missy's Music** (Kindness): all groups
11:20 – 11:35 am	Snacks (all groups)	Snacks (all groups)	Snacks (all groups)
11:40 am – 12:40 pm	**Korie's Crafts** (Faith): groups 4 and 5 **Warehouse** (Faith): groups 1, 2, and 3	**Korie's Crafts** (Prayer): groups 4 and 5 **Warehouse** (Prayer): groups 1, 2, and 3	**Korie's Crafts** (Kindness): groups 4 and 5 **Warehouse** (Kindness): groups 1, 2, and 3
12:45 – 1:45 pm	Lunch	Lunch	Lunch
1:50 – 2:30 pm (40 minutes)	**Bull Pen** (Faith): all groups	**Bull Pen** (Prayer): all groups	**Bull Pen** (Kindness): all groups
2:35 – 3:05 pm (30 minutes)	**Missy's Music** (Forgiveness): all groups	**Missy's Music** (Prayer): all groups	**Missy's Music** (free choice): all groups
3:10 – 3:55 pm (45 minutes)	**Korie's Crafts** (Forgiveness): groups 1, 2, and 3 **Warehouse** (Forgiveness): groups 4 and 5	**Korie's Crafts** (Obedience): groups 1, 2, and 3 **Warehouse** (Obedience): groups 4 and 5	**Korie's Crafts** (free choice): groups 1, 2, and 3 **Warehouse** (free choice): groups 4 and 5
4:00 – 4:45 pm (45 minutes)	**Korie's Crafts** (Forgiveness): groups 4 and 5 **Warehouse** (Forgiveness): groups 1, 2, and 3	**Korie's Crafts** (Obedience): groups 4 and 5 **Warehouse** (Obedience): groups 1, 2, and 3	**Korie's Crafts** (free choice): groups 4 and 5 **Warehouse** (free choice): groups 1, 2, and 3
4:50 – 5:20 pm (30 minutes)	**Bull Pen** (Forgiveness): all groups	**Bull Pen** (Obedience): all groups	Snacks (all groups)
5:25 – 5:45 pm	Closing Roundup	Closing Roundup	Closing Roundup

GATHERING YOUR VOLUNTEERS

As the director of Willie's Redneck Rodeo, your job is to put together a team of volunteers who are excited about sharing the message of Christ with kids! To find these talented individuals you might want to start with men and women who are currently serving your children at your church. Tweens (eleven- and twelve-year-olds) and teenagers are also a great resource and are often willing to help in many areas, from guiding students through their station rotations to leading groups.

DETERMINING YOUR VOLUNTEER NEEDS

To figure out the number of volunteers you will need, begin by writing down the number of participants you think your facility can accommodate.

> Number of participants our church can accommodate: _____

From there, you need to plan as if you will reach maximum capacity. That way, you are sure to be prepared! Indicate below the number of preschoolers, early elementary, and later elementary children you expect to register.

Total number of preschoolers
(4- to 5-year-olds): _____
Total number of early elementary
(grades K–2): _____
Total number of later elementary
(grades 3–5): _____

Now it's time for some math. Take the numbers you wrote above and use the ratios below to guesstimate how many small-group leaders you will need to help you wrangle those students without any hassles.

> *Preschool:* 3 children to 1 volunteer
> *Early Elementary:* 5 children to 1 volunteer
> *Later Elementary:* 8 children to 1 volunteer

So, for example, let's assume you identified that your facility can accommodate 100 kids. You determined that you will likely register 23 preschoolers, 44 early elementary students, and 33 later elementary students. Using the above ratios (and rounding up or down), you would need the following number of volunteers for each age group:

> *Preschool:* 8 volunteers (23 ÷ 3)
> *Early Elementary:* 9 volunteers (44 ÷ 5)
> *Later Elementary:* 4 volunteers (33 ÷ 8)

VOLUNTEER JOB DESCRIPTIONS

Once you determine how many volunteers you will require, you need to figure out which individuals to assign to which roles. Following are general descriptions of all the jobs you will need to fill.

ROUNDUP LEADER

The Roundup Leader is responsible for making sure the opening and closing sessions—called the Opening Roundup and the Closing Roundup—go off without a hitch. The Roundup leader casts the various parts needed for the skits, presents the scripts to the actors, and helps the actors rehearse their parts.

STATION LEADERS

The Station Leaders are responsible for leading the children through the activities that have been designed for their specific station. In addition, some of the station leaders will have parts in each day's skit. The following is a list of the station leaders that you will need throughout Willie's Redneck Rodeo:

- **Missy's Music and Memory Station:** This leader will play the part of Missy Robertson and will be responsible for planning and directing the music station. This includes determining which songs to teach the kids and arranging for the sound equipment that needs to be in place. The person you choose will also help the children memorize each day's verse. (See pages 99–100 for more information about this role.)

- **Korie's Craft Shed:** This leader will play the part of Korie Robertson and will be responsible for organizing and directing the craft station. This includes purchasing all necessary items, decorating the room, and determining which craft to use. The leader of this station can also participate in the opening skit on Day 3. (See pages 107–108 for more information about this role.)

- **The Warehouse:** This leader will play the part of Willie Robertson and will be responsible for organizing and directing the games for the VBS. This includes collecting all equipment needed and determining which age-appropriate games the children will play. This leader can also participate in the opening skits for each day, and coleaders could also play the parts of Jase, Jep, Martin, and Godwin in the skits. (See pages 113–114 for more information about these roles.)

- **Miss Kay's Kitchen:** This leader will play the part of Miss Kay, mother to the Robertson boys, and will be responsible for organizing and directing the snack venue. This person will work with you to determine snacks, recruit helpers, and set up the station. In addition, this leader can participate in the opening skits for Days 4 and 5. (See pages 123–124 for more information about this role.)

- **Si's Bull Pen:** This leader will play the part of Si Robertson and will be responsible for gathering materials, helpers, and needed supplies to lead the written activities for each day's activities. In addition, this leader can participate in the opening skits for each day. (See pages 135–136 for more information about this role.)

Encourage your volunteers who are acting in the skits for the Opening Roundup to also assist each of these station leaders (in costume).

OPENING ROUNDUP ACTORS

As mentioned above, your station leaders for Korie's Craft Shed, the Warehouse, Miss Kay's Kitchen, and Si's Bull Pen can also serve as actors for the opening skits. In addition to these actors, you will need to choose adult volunteers to play (and dress) the part of Phil Robertson, who will come onstage after the opening skit and present a teaching on the Bible parable for the day. You will also need actors to play the parts of Jase, Jep, Martin, Godwin, Mountain Man, Bella, John Luke, Sadie, and Will. (See pages 13–14 to give you an idea of how the main actors should dress and the costumes you should use.) Your actors can be comprised of teens or adults, but they will need to rehearse their parts prior to the Opening Roundup for the day. See each day's schedule for which actors are needed and what costumes are required.

THE ROCKIN' REDNECKS

This is your team of praise and worship leaders for the week. Have them dress in gear similar to that worn by Willie and the gang. Suggestions for songs are provided for each day, but your team is free to adapt from their personal experience. Remind your team that children love repetition, so they shouldn't be afraid to repeat songs from the day before. Consider having members of the Rockin' Rednecks participate in Missy's Music and Memory Station.

TECHNICAL CREW

The technical crew will need to set up the audio and video equipment, do sound checks, and run the soundboard.

WRANGLERS

Wranglers are adults who enjoy working with small groups of children and building relationships with them. Assign your wranglers to one group at the start of the VBS and ask them to guide the children through all the activities they will be doing at each of the stations. If you break your groups up by age, be sure to assign wranglers who are comfortable and knowledgeable about those age groups. Each wrangler should ideally have one or two rodeo hands (helpers).

RODEO HANDS

These can be tweens, teens, or adults who enjoy working with kids. Your rodeo hands will assist the wranglers (group leaders) and will help the kids move from station to station and complete the activities. In addition, you will need some rodeo hands to participate in the opening skits for each day.

RODEO REGISTRATION COORDINATOR

The rodeo registration coordinator will be responsible for registering all students and keeping accurate emergency contact information. Depending on whether your registration process is online, in person, or some combination of both, the registration coordinator may need to work with your information technology (IT) people to create online access for families. This person will also need to be on hand the first day to register last-minute walk-ins. (Note that in many churches the director of the VBS will fulfill this role.)

WELCOME TEAM

Have a few of your volunteers on hand at the start of the VBS (and on other days as needed) to do last-minute registrations, sign in and sign out the kids each day, take attendance, and help the children find their assigned groups.

SUPPORT TEAMS

Depending on the size of your VBS, you may want to recruit volunteers to serve on these additional support teams to make sure your rodeo runs without a glitch:

- Security coordinator
- Volunteer coordinator
- T-shirt coordinator
- Preschool director
- Supply coordinator
- Site decorations/creative team
- Prayer leader
- Promotion coordinator

You may also want to recruit a codirector or other right-hand person to help you get the job done!

RECRUITING TIPS

In all areas of church ministry, one of the toughest tasks for an administrator can be in recruiting volunteers. For this reason, it is critical for you to be enthusiastic about Willie's Redneck Rodeo and bringing the gospel of Christ to children so that you can transfer that same excitement to your volunteers. Creating a positive buzz will be one of the best recruiting techniques you will find. Here are a few other effective techniques you can use to get the word out about your VBS and recruit talented helpers:

- **Set up a recruiting station at your church.** Print out the promotional materials found in the "Talkin' It Up" section on pages 43–44 and set up a table at your church announcing the upcoming VBS. Man the table before and after church worship services so that the churchgoers know you are looking for volunteers. Print out a list of the job descriptions above so that people know exactly what you need. Take down contact information and get in touch with your potential volunteers during the week to follow up. Remember that personal contact is often more effective in recruiting volunteers than email, phone calls, or social media.
- **Advertise your needs on the church website and through other social media.** Many people these days use Facebook and Twitter, so be sure to contact prospective volunteers through these and other social media sites. Also post the upcoming VBS on your church's website. List your contact information and post the

job descriptions you need to fill. See page 43 for some sample social media messages.

- **Use bulletin inserts and church newsletters.** Advertise your volunteer needs in your church's bulletin or newsletter at least three weeks before your first training session.

- **Send out e-blasts.** If possible, speak with your pastor or other ministry leaders in your church and identify key individuals whom they would recommend to serve at your VBS. Obtain their email addresses and get permission to send out an e-blast to them to announce your needs. Send out your first blast at least three weeks before your first training session, and follow it up with a second blast one week before. Just make sure not to overdo the number of e-blasts you send out.

- **Ask former volunteers to talk about their VBS experience.** Ask a volunteer who has previously served in VBS to offer a testimonial to your congregation about the benefits of working with kids. These testimonials will work well during the "announcement" portion of your church's worship service. You might also want to post quotes from them about their positive experiences in any future correspondence you send to prospective volunteers and in the materials you hand out at your recruiting table.

As you begin this process, be sure not to narrow your focus down so much that you miss prospective opportunities to recruit good volunteers. For instance, teenagers and retirees will do a great job for you if they are placed in the right job descriptions. Pray each time you begin recruiting, asking God to put you in a good frame of mind and to bring the right people to you. Also pray before you speak with any potential volunteers and ask God to prepare their hearts for what you have to say.

It is a good idea to write down a short script of what you will say when you approach a potential worker. Begin with your vision of what you hope to accomplish at the VBS and what you are praying the kids will take away from the experience. Ask your friends and other volunteers to also look for talented people who could help make your VBS a success. Finally, don't be discouraged if you are turned down, as it is likely that as many people will say no to you as will say yes.

SECURITY ISSUES

To prevent any potential problems, it is highly suggested that you conduct background checks for all VBS volunteers—even teenagers. (For more on this, see "Child Safety" on page 38). Also check out the "Rodeo Resources" section on pages 157–158 for volunteer forms (including background checks). To help your children know who they can go to for help, consider having all of your volunteers wear the same shirt. You can print the *Willie's Redneck Rodeo* logo on T-shirts for a reasonable cost (see the DVD-ROM for a file of the logo).

TRAINING YOUR VOLUNTEERS

Once your team is in place, they need to feel comfortable that they can do the job, that they have the tools they need to be successful. To this end, you may need to conduct a few meetings prior to your VBS to offer your volunteers some basic training. For ideas on when to hold these meetings, refer to the "Planning Timeline" on pages 21–22.

SAMPLE MEETING AGENDA

The following is a sample agenda of some of the information you will likely want to cover with your Willie's Redneck Rodeo team.

- **Welcome:** Offer opening comments (express your appreciation for your volunteers' willingness to be there and help the kids).
- **Opening Prayer:** Ask God to lead you and bless your time together.
- **Overview of Willie's Redneck Rodeo:** Explain the theme, the rotation schedule you've chosen, how the registration process will work, how the skits and stations will work for each day, and so forth.
- **Overview of Day One:** Explain what happens at check-in and what you will need your volunteers to help you with on the first day. (At this point, you may want to assign volunteers to serve on your Welcome Team.) Next, explain in greater detail what will happen during the Opening and Closing Roundups and at each station. Basically, walk the volunteers through a typical day at Willie's Redneck Rodeo and ask if they have any questions.
- **Leading a Child to Christ:** Go over the basics of how to lead a child to Christ (see "Leading a Child to Christ" on pages 39–40).
- **Standards of Behavior:** Go over the basics of how you expect the children to behave during their time at the VBS (see "Tips for Wrangling Students Peaceably" on pages 37–38).
- **Closing:** Thank your team members again for their service, pray as a group, dismiss the volunteers, and provide your contact information should they have any additional questions.

WORKING WITH DIFFERENT AGE GROUPS

Make sure that all of your volunteers know what to expect from the different age groups who will be attending your VBS. The following are some basics they should keep in mind when working with preschoolers (four- and five-year-olds), early elementary-aged children (kindergarten through second grade), and later elementary-aged children (third through fifth grade).

PRESCHOOLERS AT A GLANCE

In general, here are some things your volunteers need to know about preschoolers before they work with them:

- **Preschoolers are concrete learners.** Preschoolers learn using their five senses. The more your leaders can incorporate taste, touch, sound, sight, and smell into their lessons, the better!
- **Preschoolers respond to praise.** Just like the rest of us, preschoolers love to hear that they're doing something well.
- **Preschoolers are copycats.** One of the best ways to extinguish an unwanted behavior in a preschooler is to praise other students who are doing what they should be doing. Preschoolers learn from each other.
- **Preschoolers have a ton of energy.** For this reason, your volunteers need to keep them moving around as much as possible. Have them change up the activities frequently so the children can get their wiggles and giggles out. It's also important to give preschoolers brief times in which they can demonstrate self-control and being still.

EARLY ELEMENTARY AT A GLANCE

In general, here are some things your volunteers need to know about early elementary-aged children before they work with them:

- **Early elementary children are improving in muscle coordination.** Your leaders need to keep in mind that there will be certain activities that might be difficult for the younger ages to perform physically. Girls tend to take the lead in this area over boys.
- **Early elementary children are more emotional.** Children in this age group might find it hard to control their emotions when things don't go their way and may throw tantrums. Your leaders need to recognize this fact and be understanding toward the kids who are having trouble.
- **Early elementary children like to please their teachers.** Make sure your leaders communicate clearly what they expect from their groups and that they praise the children frequently for a job well done.
- **Early elementary children think literally and ask many questions.** For this reason, your volunteer with this age group needs to have a lot of patience and understanding.

LATER ELEMENTARY AT A GLANCE

In general, here are some things your volunteers need to know about later elementary-aged children before they work with them:

- **Later elementary children have good small/large muscle coordination.** In the middle elementary ages the girls will still be ahead of the boys, but this discrepancy disappears by late elementary. Many of the children will be skilled in their areas of interest.
- **Later elementary children understand social groups.** Children in this age group

might form cliques and engage in excluding those not in their inner circle. Your leaders need to be aware of this fact and address it when they see it. Under no condition should they tolerate any form of bullying when they see it.

- **Later elementary children like things to be fair.** By this age, children like to know that everything is fair and that others in the group aren't receiving advantages that they are not getting.
- **Later elementary children might keep their feelings to themselves.** While middle elementary children might be more prone to show their feelings, by late elementary, kids tend to keep those feelings more to themselves. For this reason, you need a leader who is observant and can draw out a student who might be holding back.
- **Later elementary children like to be liked.** Kids in this age group like to be affirmed and be accepted for their independent thinking. They tend to work well in groups and look up to role models.
- **Later elementary children like to find the answers for themselves.** Instead of being told what to think, children in this age group like to discover the answers for themselves. Some children might even begin to question adults' opinions at this stage. Your leaders need to keep this in mind when directing their activities.

TIPS FOR WRANGLIN' STUDENTS PEACEABLY (THE RULES)

We all know that children can get out of hand if you let them. So, as a leader, you and your team need to "cut 'em off at the pass," which means to *think about what they're going to do before they do it*. Don't let your kids catch you off guard! Preventing trouble is always better than sorting out trouble after the fact. Each of your volunteers should be ready to reinforce these three simple rodeo rules:

> **1. Listen Up!** God gave your kids two ears and one mouth, so they should do twice as much listening as they do talking!
> **2. Love Up!** All of the students' words and actions should show love first and foremost!
> **3. Saddle Up!** The children who attend your VBS need to obey their wranglers and rodeo hands at all times!

If a child's behavior is unacceptable and disruptive to others, you need to remind him or her of these three rules. Let the children know ahead of time that if they do not behave in an appropriate manner they can be sent to "Duck Command" — the director's office — and then possibly sent home. The children need to understand that rodeo participation is a privilege, not a right. You are happy that they are there, but it would be unfair for you to allow their behavior to disrupt the experience of the other children who are attending. Here are some other simple guidelines to follow:

- **Be positive when giving rules.** Encourage your leaders to state the benefits the children will receive by following the rules rather than the penalties they will suffer. For example, "If you stay quiet and listen, we can all move to the next station more quickly."
- **Be respectful.** Your leaders will get more cooperation from the children if they address them in respectful and nonconfrontational

ways. For example, "When you are finished, I would really appreciate it if you could put away the crayons. Thank you!"

- **Validate the children's feelings.** Children like to know that they are being understood, even if the leaders still can't give them what they are asking. For example, "I understand that you would like another snack, but we first need to make sure everyone has had one."

- **Provide acceptable alternatives.** Ask your leaders to clarify requests, give reasons for any limitations they have to impose, and provide the children alternatives if possible. For example, "I know you want to play another round of the game, but right now Miss Kay is waiting for us at the next station. But I will tell Willie and Jase that you really enjoyed this game, and maybe you can play again tomorrow."

Work to train your wranglers and rodeo hands to defuse small problems within their groups and not allow them to escalate to the point where they are out of control. Also encourage them to handle any problem without drawing too much of the other children's attention to it. Make sure your leaders have enough helpers and support staff available to help them deal with any discipline problems that arise.

CHILD SAFETY

At Willie's Redneck Rodeo, child safety should be one of your top priorities. You want every child who comes to your rodeo to feel cared for and secure. This will help your children develop trust with your leaders, which in turn will lead to greater learning and spiritual growth. To make sure this happens, you need to consider several key points:

- **Volunteer concerns:** As previously mentioned, it is important to conduct background checks on *all* volunteers to make sure none of them have criminal backgrounds or have been involved with inappropriateness toward children. Conducting such checks will not only protect the children but also your church. Check out the "Rodeo Resources" section on pages 157–158 for volunteer forms (including background checks).

- **Site concerns:** You need to make sure the location where you will be holding the VBS is free of any potential dangers to children—such as dangerous objects, access to strangers, and other issues.

- **Registration concerns:** It is important to consider how you will make sure that your students stay with their assigned wrangler and rodeo hands throughout the day. Make sure you have a person manning the desk at the beginning of the day to check in children, and later to check them out by someone who is approved by the child's family. Don't allow someone you don't know or who is not approved to ever pick up a child from your VBS.

- **Child-to-child concerns:** Make sure that your children "do no harm" to one another. As mentioned previously, do not allow any bullying or intimidation among the children at your VBS. Also consider how you will accommodate any special dietary and physical needs that some of your students may have.

STUDENTS WITH SPECIAL NEEDS

Every child is special and deserves the chance to participate in Willie's Redneck Rodeo as fully as he or she can. So, as you consider ministering to your kids, don't overlook those children who will attend who might have special needs. Here is a brief list of what you can do to make sure these children do not feel they are being left out of the action.

- **Determine the child's special needs.** You can do this by having the parent or guardian complete the appropriate information on the registration form (see page 159).
- **Follow up with the family.** Give the child's parent or guardian a call or schedule an in-person meeting to discuss what steps need to be taken to adequately address the need. Make sure you let that person know you care, that you want his or her child to attend, and that you are taking steps to make sure the child's need is addressed.
- **Train your volunteers.** If you have a volunteer with experience in dealing with the child's special need, be sure to assign the child to that person's group. If not, you may need to conduct a training session with the volunteer (possibly in conjunction with the parent or guardian). Be sure that the wrangler and his or her rodeo hands have considered effective ways to interact with and engage the child.
- **Come up with an inclusion plan.** Depending on the type of need, you may need to come up with a plan for how you will engage the child during his or her time at the VBS. If the child has certain dietary restrictions, be sure to let the kitchen volunteers know and those leaders who are conducting the Miss Kay's Kitchen station.

LEADING A CHILD TO CHRIST

The main goal of Willie's Redneck Rodeo is to teach children (and their parents) about Jesus and help them to form a personal relationship with Him. This might sound difficult at first, but remember that it is not you and your volunteers who do the leading—it is the Lord Himself who does the ropin', wranglin', and lassoin' of a child's heart! So remind your wranglers and rodeo hands of these facts during your volunteer training session. Tell them that it is simply their job to be available to listen, talk, explain, and answer any questions their kids might have about Jesus. On the next page is a simple ABC approach you might want to share with your wranglers to better prepare them to work with the children. However, everyone who works with the children should be aware that the choice to take the next step of redonkulous faith should be entirely the children's. Please do not force a decision on the children; only allow God's Word to speak to their hearts. It would be good if your wranglers and rodeo hands kept a children's Bible with them at all times, such as the NIRV (New International Reader's Version) or the Gospel of John. This way they would have scriptures right before them as the children are seeking answers.

THE ABCS OF TRUSTING JESUS

Admit you are a sinner and **A**sk for His Holy Spirit to come into your life (Romans 3:23; 6:23; 8:9).

Believe Jesus, the Son of God, will save you and **B**e **B**aptized (Romans 10:9; 6:1–4).

Confess with your mouth Jesus is Lord and **C**ommit to **C**hanging to be more like Him (Romans 10:13; 7:24–25).

REGISTRATION AND ATTENDANCE

To get into most rodeos these days, you need a ticket. Likewise, as VBS director, it is important that you come up with a way to register all the children who want to attend your rodeo. Will your registration be online, on paper, or both? (See the sample registration form in the "Rodeo Resources" section on page 159). When will you open registration? When will you close it? Will you recruit a special "rodeo registration coordinator," or will you handle the job yourself? (See "Planning Timeline" on pages 21–22.) Regardless of what you do before the VBS begins, note that you will need to have a volunteer (or a welcome team) manning the front tables to sign up any last-minute participants, sign children in and out, and take attendance each day.

OPENING DAY

On the first day of your VBS, be prepared for kids to show up who haven't signed up in advance. Once again, it is important for your volunteers manning your front check-in tables to have hard copies of your rodeo registration form. Remember that some parents and children may be attending your church for the first time, so you want your volunteers manning the front tables to be friendly and inviting.

If you prefer, they can dress the part of the various Robertson family members or, if you chose to make *Willie's Redneck Rodeo* T-shirts, they can wear those as they check in the children. Provide extra tables where parents and guardians can complete the registration forms, and gently encourage them to fill in all of the necessary items. Remind them that your first priority is their children's safety, which is why you are requesting this information.

CHECK-IN/CHECK-OUT SHEETS

Once again, for security purposes it is vital that you have parents or guardians sign their kids in and out of the VBS. Only allow those individuals who have been preapproved on the registration form to check out the children. In addition, make sure your volunteers have plenty of help available (especially on the first day) to take care of the walk-in registrations, check off the children on the registered list, and assign them to specific groups. Keep track of the group to which the children have been assigned (see the sample Check-In/Check-Out Sheet in the "Rodeo Resources" section on page 156.) At the end of your VBS, this sign-in sheet will serve as your master attendance list so you can see who was in attendance and how many children were in each group.

GROUP NAMES

As previously noted, one great way to group children is according to age or grade. For this reason, the Check-In/Check-Out Sheet includes a column for your volunteers to record each child's age. From there, depending on the size of your VBS, you will assign the kids to a wrangler (adult volunteer) in groups of 5 to 10 kids each, and then you will assign their group a fun rodeo name.

Some fun names that you might want to consider include Barrel Racers, Cowgirls, Cowboys, Wild Broncos, Black Bulls, and Mustangs. You can also take more of a *Duck Dynasty*® approach and call the groups after the names of the main characters, such as Korie's Cadets, Willie's Wild Bunch, Jase's Jumpers, and Si's Serious Students. You can even go crazy by finding some clip art and creating logos for each "herd." The kids will love being part of a group with a special identity.

If you organize your groups by age, give the later elementary kids some of the "cooler" names such as Mustangs or Willie's Wild Bunch, as they won't want to be associated with a "babyish" name. After all, they've got a reputation to keep up.

TALKIN' IT UP [PROMOTION]

As incredible as your vision might be for how you will impact children's lives through Willie's Redneck Rodeo, nothing will ever happen unless you spread the word and let people know about your exciting VBS! Talkin' it up is a vital part to promoting your rodeo, so you need to make sure you create the right materials and get them all over town before the big event (see the "Planning Timeline" on pages 21–22). Don't forget that every great piece of promotional material should answer the six basic questions: (1) Who? (2) What? (3) When? (4) Where? (5) Why? (6) How? The following will provide you with several samples you can use or adapt to effectively promote your VBS.

SOCIAL MEDIA

TWITTER MESSAGES

• Add a redneck to a rodeo and what do you get? Willie's Redneck Rodeo! Click here to register your child for VBS! [Insert link.]

• Lookin' for somethin' for your kids to do this summer? Check out Willie's Redneck Rodeo!

• Teach your kids the parables of Jesus through the Robertson family from *Duck Dynasty*®! Sign up your kids today!

• Redneck + Rodeo + VBS + Robertson Family = FUN!

• Come to Willie's Redneck Rodeo VBS @ [insert church name and link]

Note: Consider creating a hashtag such as #WRR or #redneckrodeo to add to all your tweets.

FACEBOOK

Use the same messages as you do for Twitter but take advantage of Facebook and post a photo along with each message. For some ideas of pictures, you might want to include rodeo photos, photos of the Robertson family, Duck Commander photos (including the warehouse), or children's activity photos.

Feel free to use the following copy or create your own:

Calling all Rednecks!

The Robertson family from *Duck Dynasty*® invites you to attend

Willie's
REDNECK RODEO
LASSOING FIVE VALUES FROM THE PARABLES OF JESUS

To be held on: _____

At: _____ Cost: _____

Who: Children ages 4–12

REGISTER ONLINE OR IN PERSON BY CONTACTING:

Name: _____ Phone: _____

Website: _____

Email: _____

We're also looking for some fantastic volunteers
to help us wrangle all these kids!

If you're interested in being a Wrangler or Rodeo Hand,
give us a holler!

RODEO ROUNDUPS

THE ROUNDUP EXPERIENCE

What's a rodeo without rockin' music, "clowns," and a good show? The Roundup is a group experience that all the children will attend at the beginning and end of each day of VBS. During this time, they will be introduced to characters dressed as Willie, Jase, Jep, Phil, Si, and other Duck Commander folks and will have a time of worship led by the Rockin' Rednecks, your worship team for the VBS. Music and movement work well to get the kids to loosen up and start the day, so the Roundup will be a great way for you to get the excitement going early.

ROUNDUP ROTATION SCHEDULE

TIME	GROUP 1	GROUP 2	GROUP 3	GROUP 4	GROUP 5
9:00–9:25 am 5:30–5:55 pm	Opening Roundup	Opening Roundup	Opening Roundup	Opening Roundup	Opening Roundup
9:30–9:55 am 6:00–6:25 pm	Missy's Music and Memory	Si's Bull Pen	Miss Kay's Kitchen	The Warehouse	Korie's Craft Shed
10:00–10:25 am 6:30–6:55 pm	Korie's Craft Shed	Missy's Music and Memory	Si's Bull Pen	Miss Kay's Kitchen	The Warehouse
10:30–10:55 am 7:00–7:25 pm	The Warehouse	Korie's Craft Shed	Missy's Music and Memory	Si's Bull Pen	Miss Kay's Kitchen
11:00–11:25 am 7:30–7:55 pm	Miss Kay's Kitchen	The Warehouse	Korie's Craft Shed	Missy's Music and Memory	Si's Bull Pen
11:30–11:55 am 8:00–8:25 pm	Si's Bull Pen	Miss Kay's Kitchen	The Warehouse	Korie's Craft Shed	Missy's Music and Memory
12:00–12:15 am 8:30–8:45 pm	Closing Roundup	Closing Roundup	Closing Roundup	Closing Roundup	Closing Roundup

SETTING THE STAGE

Consider holding the Roundups in one of the largest spaces at your site. This central location will serve as the starting point each day, and it will be where your kids will check in with their wranglers (group leaders) and rodeo hands (group helpers).

The only set you need for the Roundup is one decorated like the Duck Call Shop from the television show. Set up a simple wooden desk on the stage and put some office chairs around it. Place some smaller boxes on the desk along with the typical office-type clutter and pile larger cardboard boxes in the area. Label the boxes "Duck Calls" and/or place smaller boxes on the top filled with whistles or anything that looks like duck calls. On the back wall put up a large sign that reads "Duck Commander" and hang some smaller pictures of all the guys.

Make the set as elaborate as you like, but be sure to preserve the workshop-type feel that is represented in the show. Position the Duck Call shop to the right of the center stage. The characters will begin each day by addressing the audience from center stage, and then the action will move to the Duck Call Shop.

OPENING ROUNDUP SCHEDULE

Generally, you will want to allow 25 minutes for the Opening Roundup time, though you can tailor this to whatever works best for your VBS. If you are using the suggested schedule, the following is a sample of how you could plan your time.

TIME	ACTIVITY
9:00–9:05	Opening Music
9:05–9:10	Welcome and Share
9:10–9:18	Introduction/Worship Time
9:18–9:25	Skit and Bible Lesson
9:25	Duck Call Dismissal

OPENING MUSIC
5 MINUTES

Have music playing as the children enter the main room.

WELCOME AND SHARE
(5 MINUTES)

When you are ready to begin, welcome the children to the event and have everyone stand for an opening prayer. Spend some time asking two or three of the kids to explain what they hope to get out of the day or what they remember from the day before. Remember to make this a fun and high-energy time! Help build the children's energy and excitement for the activities in store for them.

INTRODUCTION/ WORSHIP TIME
8 MINUTES

After the time of sharing is over, your actors portraying the Robertson family members (and characters from the show) will introduce themselves and the main theme of the day. They will invite the Rockin' Rednecks to come forward to lead the children in singing two or three high-energy songs.

SKIT AND BIBLE LESSON
7 MINUTES

Your volunteer actors will return to the stage and act out a skit that highlights the parable for the day. After this, a character dressed as Phil will read the parable from the Bible to the group. This will reinforce the lesson for the day and prepare the kids for the various stations they will next be attending.

DUCK CALL DISMISSAL

Willie and the gang will blow duck calls to send children on to their rotations. (Allow five minutes for the kids to get to their first station of the day.)

CLOSING ROUNDUP SCHEDULE

The Closing Roundup is an optional activity based on your time constraints for the VBS or children's ministry nights. If you do choose to do the Closing Roundup, it can serve as a fun way to finish off the day and reinforce the lessons the children learned, and it can bring the children to a central location for their parents to pick them up. The following is a sample for how you could plan this time.

TIME	ACTIVITY
12:00–12:05	Opening Music
12:05–12:13	Share Stories/Testimonials
12:14–12:15	Closing Prayer and Dismissal

OPENING MUSIC
5 MINUTES

Have some fun music playing to welcome the children back into the large meeting space. Allow some time for the kids to settle down from the activities of the day.

SHARE STORIES/ TESTIMONIALS
8 MINUTES

Once everyone is back in the room, either you or one of your group leaders can wrap up the day. Share some stories of what you saw that day, or ask the children to share a few stories or testimonials of what they experienced.

CLOSING PRAYER AND DISMISSAL
2 MINUTES

Wrap up the day with a few closing words, and end in prayer.

DAY ONE
REDONKULOUS FAITH

MAIN IDEA: Following God requires a "redonkulous" amount of faith!

MEMORY VERSE: 1 Corinthians 16:13

> *Preschool and Early Elementary:* "Be on your guard. Stand firm in the faith."
>
> *Later Elementary:* "Be on your guard. Stand firm in the faith. Be brave. Be strong."

BIBLE STORY: The Parable of the Sower (Matthew 13:1–23).

SUGGESTED SONGS: "By Faith" from *Under God* by Jeff Slaughter (Indie Music); "King of the Jungle" from *Great Worship Songs for Kids*, vol. 1 (Brentwood Benson).

OPENING ROUNDUP

As the children arrive for their first day of VBS, have your welcome team greet them and assign them to their groups. Make sure your rodeo hands are available and ready to sit with the children as they arrive for the opening show. Latecomers will straggle in and need to be helped to find their groups, but try to start the Opening Roundup right on time so the rest of the day's events run close to schedule.

As the children arrive and get settled into their groups, have your worship and praise music playing in the background. At the scheduled start time, provide some opening remarks, lay the ground rules for the children's behavior during the VBS (what is acceptable and what is not), and tell them that this week they will be spending some time with Willie and the rest of the Robertson gang at Willie's Redneck Rodeo. Encourage them to participate in all of the stations and get them fired up for a great week of fun! After your opening comments, your actors will come on stage to perform the skit.

PROPS

Sign that says, "One Hour Later"

CHARACTERS AND COSTUMES

JASE (black stocking cap and clothing, long brown hair, brown beard)

WILLIE (bandana, long hair, brown beard, plaid shirt)

SI (camo cap, T-shirt, camo shirt, glasses, gray beard, carries plastic cup)

PHIL (long gray beard, camo headband, camo clothes)

JEP (bandana, long hair, brown beard, plaid shirt/T-shirt)

MARTIN (baseball cap or stocking cap, camo clothes, brown beard)

GODWIN (baseball cap, camo clothes, white beard—not full)

RODEO HELPER/STAGE HAND (to walk across the stage with the sign)

SCRIPT

Jase and Willie walk out on center stage and face the audience.

JASE: Welcome, y'all! How's my redneck friends today?

WILLIE: Are y'all ready for your first day at the Redneck Rodeo?

JASE: Today we are going to talk about "redonkulous faith."

SI: Where's the donkey? Are you riding the donkey in this rodeo?

WILLIE: Si, are you crazy? We didn't say that.

SI: You said someone was gonna ride a donkey in the rodeo.

JASE: Si! We did not say that.

WILLIE: We said we were going to learn about *redonkulous* faith today.

SI: Re-who-le-ous?

JASE: Redonkulous!

SI: Re-muck-a-lus?

WILLIE: Forget it, Si! Let's just sing. Everybody stand up, and let's praise God!

The Rockin' Rednecks come out and lead a few worship songs (refer to Rockin' Rednecks suggested praise music at the beginning of Day 1).

SI: I still wanna know who's riding the donkey in the rodeo.

WILLIE AND JASE: No one, Si!

WILLIE: We are learning about faith today.

JASE: We are learning how to stand strong in our faith and always be on guard.

SI: Wellll … back in 'Nom I was on guard …

JASE: Oh, boy, here we go!

WILLIE: GET OUT OF HERE, SI! You're killin' me!

Si exits the stage. Phil enters from the other side.

PHIL: It sounds like you boys need some help. Ol' Si has a good heart, but he can cause problems with the best of 'em sometimes. We will get to *that* story in a minute. *(Turns to face the kids.)* But first, I need to ask you all a question. Do you kids know what a "parable" is? Well, a parable is an earthly story with a heavenly meaning. Ol' Si is good at telling stories, and Jesus was a good storyteller as well. Jesus used stories to teach people about God. This week, we are going to study some of these parables and learn how to have a heart like God.

We'll start today by talking about faith. Now, in the Bible, Jesus talked about seeds a few times to explain faith. One seed He mentioned was a mustard seed, which is very small. Jesus said that if we have faith even the size of a mustard seed, we can do what our minds say is impossible. Now, whether or not these "seeds of faith" grow will depend on us. Let's watch this next story to see how this works.

The action moves across the stage, where Si, Martin, Godwin, Jep, and Jase are working in the Duck Call Shop. Willie enters the shop.

SI: Boss Hog!

WILLIE: Pipe down, Si! All right, here is the deal. A major company is bringing in the whole line of our duck calls, so I really need all your best work to show them the variety we have. This is a big order, so this is gonna take teamwork and dedication. All right, I'll be back in a few minutes. I have a conference call with their head guy to finalize the delivery schedule.

SI: Teamwork? Dedication? I'm gonna need a nap, Jack!

MARTIN: He gone!

The Rodeo Helper/Stage Hand walks across with the sign that says, "One Hour Later."

MARTIN: How many duck calls did Willie say we need to make?

GODWIN: You know, I don't remember him sayin'.

JEP: Well, this seems like enough.

MARTIN: Yeah, and besides, my stomach is growlin'.

JASE: Your stomach is *always* growlin.' You can't fill that thing up.

GODWIN: I'm hungry too.

JEP: Yeah, let's go.

JASE: What about the order? Willie said it had to be done today.

MARTIN: Well, my stomach is sayin' it needs to be fed today!

JASE: I'm stayin'.

JEP: Jase, are you telling me that you are gonna miss out on lunch?

JASE: Well ... I don't want to miss lunch. Godwin, what are you gonna do?

GODWIN: I'm stayin'.

JASE: Maybe I should stay and work too ...

JEP: Seriously? You are gonna stay here and miss out on the pizza buffet just to finish up some duck calls for Willie?

JASE: Well, when you put it like that, I'm gone.

JEP: Godwin?

GODWIN: I'm still stayin'.

MARTIN: All right, Godwin, you finish up Willie's order while we are gone!

Jase, Jep, and Martin all laugh and exit. The Rodeo Helper/Stage Hand walks across with the sign that says, "One Hour Later." Willie enters the Duck Call Shop.

WILLIE: Godwin? Where is everyone?

GODWIN: Wellll …

WILLIE: Have you been here workin' all alone on all these duck calls?

GODWIN: Yep!

WILLIE: Well, come on! Miss Kay just called, and she is laying out a huge feast with all of our favorite foods. She invited us to come, eat, and enjoy.

GODWIN: We gone!

Willie and Godwin leave the stage. Phil walks out holding his Bible.

PHIL: Our story today is based on the Parable of the Sower, and it is found in Matthew chapter 13. Let me read this story to you.

A farmer went out to plant his seed. He scattered the seed on the ground. Some fell on a path. Birds came and ate it up. Some seed fell on rocky places, where there wasn't much soil. The plants came up quickly, because the soil wasn't deep. When the sun came up, it burned the plants. They dried up because they had no roots. Other seed fell among thorns. The thorns grew up and crowded out the plants. Still other seed fell on good soil. It produced a crop 100, 60 or 30 times more than what was planted. Those who have ears should listen (Matthew 13:3–9).

Now, here is what Jesus said this parable means.

People hear the message about the kingdom but do not understand it. Then the evil one comes. He steals what was planted in their hearts. Those people are like the seed planted on a path. Others received the seed that fell on rocky places. They are those who hear the message and at once receive it with joy. But they have no roots. So they last only a short time. They quickly fall away from the faith when trouble or suffering comes because of the message. Others received the seed that fell among the thorns. They are those who hear the message. But then the worries of this life and the false promises of wealth crowd it out. They keep it from producing fruit. But still others received the seed that fell on good soil. They are those who hear the message and understand it. They produce a crop 100, 60 or 30 times more than the farmer planted (Matthew 3:19–23).

You see, God's Word is like a seed that is planted in the soil of our hearts, and the state of our hearts will determine whether that seed grows or dies. If our hearts are hard like the path in this story, we won't be able to understand God's Word. The seed of faith will just sit on the surface. Soon, the evil one—that's the devil, who is always prowling around—will come and take that seed away. Our faith will not get the chance to grow.

Now, if our hearts are like the rocky soil, we might hear God's Word and get all excited about it, but that's about all we will do. Those seeds of faith won't sink in deep and develop strong roots. Because of this, when trouble or suffering comes our way, our faith won't last. We will drift away instead of turning to God for help.

What if our hearts are like the soil with thorns? Well, in this case we will hear God's Word and believe what it says, but when the daily worries come—or we get distracted with the things in this life—God's Word will get pushed out. Those worldly things will take over our hearts, and before long there will be nothing left of our faith.

Ah, but if our hearts are like the good soil in this story, then we will hear God's Word, try to understand it, and put it into practice. In this good soil, those seeds of faith will take root and grow, and each time we see God working in our lives, our faith will grow even more. Before long we will have a faith that will allow us to stand strong against the work of the devil. That's redonkulous faith!

Now, in our skit today, Si, Martin, Jep, and Jase all got distracted from making those duck calls for Willie. They decided it was more important to follow their stomachs than to follow what Willie had asked them to do. They were like the people in Jesus's parable who had hard, rocky, or thorny hearts. Godwin is the only one who stayed behind and kept working. He is like the people in Jesus's parable who had good-soil hearts. He ended up getting rewarded with a super good meal at Miss Kay's, just like we will get rewarded when we allow redonkulous faith to grow in our hearts. Now, I think I hear Willie and the gang returning from lunch.

Willie and the gang come out blowing duck calls. Si comes out riding a stick horse.

SI: Yeeehaaaw! I'm ready, Willie. I got this. Yeeehaaaw!

WILLIE: Si! You would do better at wearin' a clown suit than ridin' a donkey. *(Turns to audience.)* All right, kids! WOW! That was a great lesson on standing firm and having a heart ready to accept God's Word and grow in faith. Now you are going to break into groups and have fun with some of my favorite people. Let's all remember to go crazy redneck up in here for Jesus!

Duck calls blow and music plays as the kids head out to their stations.

CLOSING ROUNDUP

Have the music playing as the children return from their final station. Once everyone is back in the room, say a few words to wrap up the day's events, or have one of your group leaders (or the character dressed as Phil) do the recap. The following is a sample script that you can follow.

SCRIPT

So, did y'all have a great time at Willie's Redneck Rodeo today? *(The kids respond, "Yes!")* Great!

Now, who can tell me what it means to have "redonkulous faith"? *(Let the kids respond.)* That's right — it means having a ridiculous amount of faith. You know, your faith can start out as small as a tiny mustard seed, but if you tend to it, it will grow and grow until it is as powerful as a mighty wind! That's redonkulous faith! So, how can you "tend" to your seed of faith? *(By reading the Bible, praying, sharing our faith with others, believing in God, and always doing what He tells us to do.)* That's right!

Having faith in God simply means trusting that He is your

defender, deliverer, and provider. It's like Miss Kay when she follows a recipe. Miss Kay has some recipes that she has used over and over, so she knows that when she puts all the ingredients together, it will turn into something tasty and good. She has faith in that recipe because she has seen it turn out well in the past. But if a friend gives Miss Kay a *brand new* recipe that Miss Kay has never tried before, she *really* has to have faith that it will turn out yummy! She doesn't know for sure, but she trusts her friend, so she has faith in the recipe.

The same is true with God. When we see Him do things again and again for us, we will begin to realize we can always depend on Him, and that knowledge will make our faith grow stronger. But there will be some things that happen to us that we have never experienced before. In those situations, we may have to stretch our faith a bit and just believe that God can handle it.

Okay, so who would like to share a story of what you learned today about redonkulous faith, or about a time in your life where you had to stretch your faith and believe God would come through for you? *(Allow the children to share as time allows, or share a few personal stories of things you observed today or how God has stretched your faith in the past.)*

CLOSING PRAYER AND DISMISSAL

Thank the children who shared their stories with the group. Close by expressing your gratitude to God for giving us His Word, the Bible. Ask God to continue to help the children have hearts that represent "good soil"—hearts that seek to understand how He wants them to live and grow in redonkulous faith. Here is a sample prayer you can use:

Dear God, thank You so much for Your Word, the Bible. Help us to be "good soil" and have hearts that seek to understand how You want us to live. Help us to always do what You want us to do. We want to grow up strong in our faith to serve You. In Jesus's name, Amen.

Tell the children that tomorrow's theme will be on forgiveness, so they need to make sure they come back for more fun at Willie's Redneck Rodeo!

DAY TWO
RADICAL FORGIVENESS

MAIN IDEA: God wants us to forgive others in a radical way!

MEMORY VERSE: Colossians 3:13

> *Preschool and Early Elementary:* "Forgive, just as the Lord forgave you."
>
> *Later Elementary:* "Put up with each other. Forgive the things you are holding against one another. Forgive, just as the Lord forgave you."

BIBLE STORY: The Parable of the Unmerciful Servant (Matthew 18:21–35)

SUGGESTED SONGS: "His Great Love" from *Pandamania* VBS (Group Publishing); "Revelation Song" from *Great Worship Songs for Kids*, vol. 5 (Brentwood Benson).

OPENING ROUNDUP

As the children arrive and get settled into their groups, have your Rockin' Rednecks leading songs up front or some other worship and praise music playing in the background. At the scheduled start time, provide some opening remarks, remind the children about the ground rules for their behavior during the VBS, and encourage them to participate in all of the stations. After your opening comments, the actors will come on stage to perform the skit.

CHARACTERS AND COSTUMES

MOUNTAIN MAN (camo cap and clothing, gray beard)

SI (camo cap, T-shirt, camo shirt, glasses, gray beard, carries plastic cup)

WILLIE (bandana, long hair, brown beard, plaid shirt)

JEP (bandana, long hair, brown beard, plaid shirt/T-shirt)

MARTIN (baseball cap or stocking cap, camo clothes, brown beard)

GODWIN (baseball cap, camo clothes, white beard—not full)

PHIL (long gray beard, camo headband, camo clothes)

SCRIPT

Mountain Man walks out on center stage and faces the audience.

MOUNTAIN MAN *(talking slowly)*: Welcome, Rednecks! Wellll ... y'all ready? ... Now, as you might remember from yesterday, this week we are learning about how to have a heart like God's heart. So, let's bring out once again our Rockin' Rednecks to help us worship and praise our God.

The Rockin' Rednecks come out and lead a few worship songs (refer to Rockin' Rednecks suggested praise music at the beginning of Day 2).

MOUNTAIN MAN: That's some goood singin'! Now, I suppose y'all are wondering why I'm here. Weeelll ... I came here today to tell you a story.

Si walks out onto the stage. Phil enters from the other side.

SI: Hey, Jack! Wait a minute—I'm the storyteller!

MOUNTAIN MAN: Weeelll ... I don't know ...

SI: I know you don't know. Mountain Man, I'm the one who is gonna tell the story today, not you! *(Turns to the audience.)* Okay, you ready, kids? You see it goes like this ...

PHIL: Hold up, Si! Before we get too far into the story, I want to make sure everyone remembers what a "parable" is. *(Turns to the* *audience.)* Who can remember from yesterday? *(Let a few of the children in the audience respond.)* That's right — a parable is an earthly story with a heavenly meaning. Jesus was a good storyteller, and He used parables to teach people about God. Now, who can tell me what we learned about yesterday? Redonkulous … *(Let a few kids respond.)* Yep, redonkulous faith. Even if we have faith the size of a tiny mustard seed, God can make it grow to a redonkulous size. *(Turns to Si.)* Okay, Si, go ahead and tell your story.

SI: All right, it starts like this. You see, in the Duck Call Shop …

MOUNTAIN MAN *(faces the Duck Call Shop and puts his hand on his brow as if he if looking off in the distance)*: Where? I don't see anything …

SI *(ignoring Mountain Man)*: Now, where's my tea glass? I can't tell my story without my tea glass …

PHIL: Boys, how 'bout we just go show 'em?

SI: Hey, that's a great idea. Kids, y'all wanna go to the Duck Call Shop? *(Kids respond, "Yay!")* All right, let's go.

Si, Mountain Man, and Phil walk offstage. The action moves to the set decorated like the Duck Call Shop. Martin, Godwin and Jep are working there. Willie enters.

WILLIE: Hey, Jep, I need to get my fishing rod back from you. John Luke wants me to take him out on the boat tomorrow, so I need it.

JEP: About that …

WILLIE: What do you mean *about that?*

JEP: It wasn't a good fishing rod anyway.

WILLIE: Are you crazy? That was my favorite rod … the Viper3000. I caught the fish of all fish on that pole.

Martin holds out his hands to indicate the size of the fish. Godwin shakes his head and pushes Martin's hands together to make the fish smaller.

WILLIE: Knock it off, you two.

JEP: I lost it, man. I think I must have left it on the bank when I was getting River and all his gear in the truck.

WILLIE: Jep! Are you kidding me?

JEP: I'm sorry, man. I'll get you another one.

WILLIE: Another one? I want that one — the one I caught the "beast" with!

MARTIN *(to Godwin)***:** Now it's a "beast" instead of a fish.

JEP: I'm really sorry, man. I'll get you another one.

WILLIE: Well, all right. That's okay, man. I forgive you … guess I'll go borrow Jase's.

Willie exits.

JEP: Whew! I was worried about that!

Si walks in.

GODWIN: Well, it's about time …

SI: Hey, Jack!

MARTIN: Where have you been … nappin'?

SI: Only a short one.

JEP: Hey, Si, where's my coffee cup?

SI: Your what?

JEP: My camo coffee cup!

SI: I don't have your camo coffee cup.

JEP: Yeah, you do. I let you use it the other day when your tea cup went MIA.

SI: Oh, that piece of junk? I don't know what I did with that … but it STUNK. It made my tea taste terrible.

JEP *(getting irritated)***:** Yeah, I know it stunk, but that was MY coffee cup, and I need it.

GODWIN: You need to calm down, Jep.

MARTIN: You don't even drink coffee out of that cup.

GODWIN: All you do is keep your ink pens in it. You don't ever use it.

JEP *(yelling)***:** That is not the point! It is MINE, and I want it back!

Willie enters.

WILLIE: What is going on in here? I could hear y'all from way back in my office. It doesn't take that kinda noise to make duck calls.

MARTIN: Jep is going after Si 'cause Si took his coffee cup and didn't return it.

WILLIE: That piece of junk? Jep, you don't even drink coffee out of that cup.

JEP: That's NOT the point!

WILLIE: Well, what I see is . . . you need to forgive Si! I forgave you, Jep, for losing my Viper3000 fishing rod. Are you telling me you can't forgive Si for losing a coffee cup you don't even use?

JEP *(hangs his head)***:** I see your point. I'm sorry, Si. I forgive you.

WILLIE: All right, boys . . . back to work! You got duck calls to build!

SI: Anybody seen my tea cup?

The actors remain in the Duck Call Shop as the action moves to center stage. Phil walks out holding his Bible to give the lesson.

PHIL: What you just saw, my little brothers and sisters, reminds me of a parable that Jesus told. It is called the Parable of the Unmerciful Servant, and it is found in the Bible in Matthew chapter 18. Jesus told this story to teach us how God wants us to forgive others—how we should have "radical forgiveness." Now, who here knows what "radical" means? *(Allow a few of the kids in the audience to respond.)* Well, it means forgive in such a way that others might not understand it! In fact, they might think we are crazy for forgiving others that way! Let me read the story to you.

A king . . . wanted to collect all the money his servants owed him. As the king began to do it, a man who owed him millions of dollars was brought to him. The man was not able to pay. So his master gave an order. The man, his wife, his children, and all he owned had to be sold to pay back what he owed.

The servant fell on his knees in front of him. "Give me time," he begged. "I'll pay everything back." His master felt sorry for him. He forgave him what he owed and let him go. But then that servant went out and found one of the other servants who owed him a few dollars. He grabbed him and began to choke him. "Pay back what you owe me!" he said.

The other servant fell on his knees. "Give me time," he begged him. "I'll pay you back." But the first servant refused. Instead, he went and had the man thrown into prison. The man would be held there until he could pay back what he owed. The other servants saw what had happened. It troubled them greatly. They went and told their master everything that had happened.

Then the master called the first servant in. "You evil servant," he said. "I forgave all that you owed me because you begged me to. Shouldn't you have had mercy on the other servant just as I had mercy on you?" In anger his master turned him over to the jailers. He would be punished until he paid back everything he owed.

This is how my Father in heaven will treat each of you unless you forgive your brother from your heart (Matthew 18:23 – 35).

That's a pretty rough story, but Jesus had a reason for telling it. He wants all of us to know that God takes forgiving others very seriously. He wants us to have radical forgiveness for others!

In today's skit, Jep lost Willie's fishing pole — and not just any fishing pole, but the one he had used to catch "the fish of all fish." Willie was sad to lose his favorite fishing rod, but he decided to forgive Jep. Willie was like the king in Jesus's parable who forgave the servant who owed him millions of dollars. Now, who was Jep like in the parable? *(Let the kids respond.)* Yep, he was like the servant who had been forgiven by the king. When Jep found out that Si had lost his camo coffee cup — a cup that he didn't even use — he got really mad at Si. But then Jep realized that if Willie could forgive him for losing his favorite fishing pole . . . well, he could find it in his heart to forgive ol' Si.

We might say Jep let Si "off the hook." Of course, when we're fishin' we want to keep the fish *on* the hook. But when we forgive others, we want to let 'em *off* the hook. Now, does this mean it will always be easy to forgive others? *(Let the kids respond.)* No way. It takes courage—not just a warm and fuzzy feeling—to decide to forgive someone. When we forgive others, do we forget about what was done to us? *(Let the kids respond.)* No, forgiving doesn't mean forgetting. God wants us to forgive others when they do something to hurt us, but that doesn't mean we allow that to happen to us again. Does forgiving others mean keeping the hurt to ourselves? *(Let the kids respond.)* Absolutely not! Our feelings are important, and we should always tell someone if a person has hurt us or if we feel sad about how others have treated us.

Each of us needs God's forgiveness in our lives, and each of us needs to radically forgive others. In my case, I know I was a pretty rough character at one point in my life. I wasn't following God. I was a bad husband to my wife and a pretty bad father to my children. But God forgave me, and He welcomed me back into His church. My wife and kids also forgave me. In the same way, God forgives all of us—and because He forgives us, He expects us to forgive others.

Willie and the gang come out blowing duck calls.

WILLIE: All right, kids, we had a great lesson today about forgiveness. Now it's time to get with your groups and go to your breakout stations. Have a great time learning about how to have radical forgiveness for others!

Duck calls blow and music plays as the kids head out to their stations.

CLOSING ROUNDUP

Have the music playing as the children return from their final station. Once everyone is back in the room, say a few words to wrap up the day's events, or have one of your group leaders (or the character dressed as Phil) do the recap. The following is a sample script that you can follow.

SCRIPT

So, did y'all have a great time at Willie's Redneck Rodeo today? *(The kids respond, "Yes!")* Great!

Now, who here can tell me what "radical forgiveness" means? *(Let the kids respond.)* That's right—it means to forgive in such a way that others might not understand it! In fact, they might think we are *crazy* for forgiving others that way. Like when someone hurts you or embarrasses you. Rather than being really mean and trying to hurt that person back, you choose to forgive him or her. You let that person off the hook.

Every family has to learn to forgive one another, or they couldn't live together. That is certainly true in the Robertson family. One time when Jase and Willie were young, they got into a big fight over the oven. Willie wanted to cook some toast, but Jase wanted to cook his frozen pizza. They got so mad at each other that a friend had to step in and remind them that they weren't acting like Christians. After a while, they both apologized and forgave each other.

That is how God calls each of us to be. Whether we're at school, or playing with our friends, or hard at work in the Duck Call Shop, we need to forgive others. We want—and need—God's forgiveness every day, and so we must be radical in the way we forgive those who wrong us. Remember that when we choose to forgive others, we're taking them off of our hook, but not saying their choices were okay. They might still have consequences for their bad choices—but we let God take care of it. When we forgive others, it helps us feel God's love and forgiveness . . . and that makes us happy, happy, happy!

Okay, so who would like to share a story of what you learned today about radical forgiveness, or about a time in your life when you had to forgive someone even though it was REALLY hard to do so? *(Allow the children to share as time allows, or share a few personal stories of things you observed today or how you have had to forgive others in the past.)*

CLOSING PRAYER AND DISMISSAL

Thank the children who shared their stories with the group. Close by expressing your gratitude to God for giving us His Word, the Bible. Ask God to continue to help the children have hearts that are able to radically forgive one another, just as God has forgiven them. Here is a sample prayer you can use:

Dear God, thank You so much for forgiving us for our sins. Help us to forgive others who hurt us. We want to forgive others just like You forgive us. We love You, God. In Jesus's name, Amen.

Tell the children that tomorrow's theme will be on prayer, so they need to make sure they come back for more fun at Willie's Redneck Rodeo!

DAY THREE RAVENOUS PRAYER

MAIN POINT: God tells us in the Bible that we are to be persistent—or "ravenous"—in prayer!

MEMORY VERSE: Philippians 4:6

Preschool and Early Elementary: "Tell God about everything. Ask and pray. Give thanks to him."

Later Elementary: "Don't worry about anything. Instead, tell God about everything. Ask and pray. Give thanks to him."

BIBLE STORY: The Parable of the Friend in Need (Luke 11:5–10).

SUGGESTED SONGS: "Watching Over You" from *Favorite VBS Songs for Families* (Group Publishing); "Great Big God" from *Great Big God* (Kids Vineyard Worship UK).

OPENING ROUNDUP

As the children arrive and get settled into their groups, have your Rockin' Rednecks leading songs up front or some other worship and praise music playing in the background. At the scheduled start time, provide some opening remarks, remind the children about the ground rules for their behavior during the VBS, and encourage them to participate in all of the stations. Note that you will need additional props for this skit and a volunteer standing by to turn off the lights. After your opening comments, the actors will come on stage to perform it.

PROPS

- Five cots, air mattresses, or folding beds. Set these up in front of the Duck Call Shop to represent Willie's house at night. Set the cots apart from each other a bit to represent different "rooms."
- Blankets for each of the characters and nightcaps for them to wear.
- Clown wigs and noses.

CHARACTERS AND COSTUMES

MARTIN (baseball cap or stocking cap, camo clothes, brown beard)

GODWIN (baseball cap, camo clothes, white beard—not full)

JEP (bandana, long hair, brown beard, plaid shirt/T-shirt)

SI (camo cap, T-shirt, camo shirt, glasses, gray beard, carries plastic cup)

JASE (black stocking cap and clothing, long brown hair, brown beard)

WILLIE (bandana, long hair, brown beard, plaid shirt)

PHIL (long gray beard, camo headband, camo clothes)

KORIE (long blond hair)

BELLA (teen actor—no special costume required)

JOHN LUKE (teen actor—no special costume required)

SADIE (teen actor—no special costume required)

WILL (teen actor—no special costume required)

RODEO HELPER/STAGE HAND (to turn off the lights)

SCRIPT

Martin, Godwin, and Jep walk to the center stage. Martin blows his duck call, and then Godwin blows one as if he is answering back. Jep blows one like he is answering Godwin, and finally Si comes out blowing one like crazy (almost as if he is talking in "duck speak"). Jase steps into all the chaos and covers his ears.

JASE: Ahh! What is going on here?

GODWIN: Well … you know how people have been sayin' that at Duck Commander we speak foul language?

JASE *(to audience)*: That's DUCK language—you know "fowl" like birds—not bad language. Anyway, go on, Godwin.

GODWIN: Wellll … we were thinking that if the ducks heard us calling them all the time, they would get used to us and come around more.

JASE *(stares in shock for a moment at Godwin, and then turns to the audience)*: Oh boy, not sure what to do with that one.

JEP: We decided to be *smart* and read ahead in the lesson. It said to talk to God all the time and He will hear us and answer. So we thought …

JASE: Hmm … let me guess. You "thought" that because in this lesson God tells us to talk with Him all the time and He will answer us, you could also talk to the ducks all the time—and they will answer you?

GODWIN: He got it too!

The guys blow the duck calls to celebrate. Jase just shakes his head.

JASE: Fellows, how do I explain this? Today we're learning about talking to *GOD* in *prayer* and how He answers us. It's different than talking to ducks. *(The guys look confused.)* Oh, never mind. Let's just sing. Come on, kids!

The Rockin' Rednecks come out and lead a few worship songs (refer to Rockin' Rednecks suggested praise music at the beginning of Day 3). The guys blow the duck calls during some of the songs. After the last song Willie comes out to center stage.

WILLIE: What is all the commotion about out here?

JASE *(hanging his head in disbelief)*: I don't even want to tell you what these clowns are doing. Just tell them to go and make some duck calls.

WILLIE: Hey! All of you get back to work! And quit trying to play a song with those duck calls! Bunch of clowns is right. I'd like to put them in the arena with my buckin' bull. He would get after them!

JASE: What? You don't have a buckin' bull.

WILLIE: Well ... if I did, he would get one of those clowns right in the hind parts.

JASE *(thinks for a moment)***:** Hey, Willie, I bet you couldn't even *ride* a bull.

WILLIE: I bet I could ride one longer than you.

JASE: Is that a challenge?

WILLIE: You're on! I know a guy who owns a buckin' bull who lives right down the road. We'll see who can ride him the longest.

JASE: Fine, but you go first. You'll be dead in eight seconds, and I'll win.

WILLIE: I can do anything for eight seconds.

Phil walks out onto the stage.

PHIL: Whoa, boys! No one is going to go ridin' a buckin' bull. You know, today's lesson is about prayer, and I'll bet that if I was to put you in a bull pen—much less on the back of a buckin' bull—I'd hear a whole lot of fervent prayer outta you. And it wouldn't take no eight seconds for you to start.

WILLIE *(mumbling)***:** Yeah, I suppose you're right.

JASE *(mumbling)***:** Be pretty stupid to climb on a buckin' bull anyway.

Willie and Jase walk away. Willie will need to circle behind the stage as Phil talks and lay down on the cot in front of the Duck Call Shop.

PHIL *(shakes his head and turns to the audience)***:** You know, both of these boys are competitive, but they are brothers. In fact, they are not only brothers because they are in the same family, but also because they are brothers in Christ. They would do anything for each other. It reminds me of a story ... but before we get to that, let's take a moment to review. Now, each day this week we are looking at a different parable that Jesus told. Who can remind me what a "parable" is? *(Let a few kids in the audience respond.)* Yes, it is an earthly story with a heavenly meaning. What did we learn about the first day? Redonkulous ... *(Let a few kids respond.)* Yep, redonkulous faith. And what did we learn about yesterday? Radical ... *(Let a few kids respond.)* Radical forgiveness. Forgiveness is at the center of God's heart. Okay, let's get to that story now.

Phil walks off the stage and the action moves to Willie's house at night. Willie, Korie, Bella, Sadie, and John Luke are all lying on the cots.

WILLIE: Night, Bella!

BELLA: Night, Mama!

KORIE: Night, Will!

WILL: Night, John Luke!

JOHN LUKE: Night, Sadie!

SADIE: Night, Dad!

Willie blows a duck call twice, and the person manning the lights turns them off. Someone offstage knocks on a door three times.

SADIE: What was that, Dad?

WILLIE: I think a tree branch just fell on the house ... go to sleep.

There are three more knocks on the door.

KORIE: Willie, you should go check who's at the door.

There are three more knocks on the door ... louder this time.

JASE (*calling from offstage*): Willie! Willie! Wake up ... it's me, Jase! I need your help.

WILLIE: Just ignore him ... nobody move ...

There are three even louder knocks on the door.

JASE: Willie! Some friends stopped by late, and we are studying the Bible with them. You know we've been redoing the kitchen and have no food to give them!

WILLIE: I'm in bed, Jase! Go away! All the kids are asleep!

JOHN LUKE: I'm not asleep!

BELLA: Really, Dad?

The knocking sound continues.

JASE: Willie! Answer the door!

KORIE: Wiiillliiieee...

WILLIE: Oh, all right!

Willie gets up and opens the door. Korie follows him. Jase enters.

WILLIE: What do you want, Jase? It's midnight and my whole family was asleep.

KORIE: Hey, Jase.

BELLA, JOHN LUKE, SADIE, AND WILL: Hey, Jase!

WILLIE: Well ... we *were* asleep until you woke us up.

JASE: Hey, sorry to come over so late, but we are having an awesome Bible study with some friends who stopped by. But they are hungry and need some food.

WILLIE: All right, come in and get whatever ya need. I'm going back to bed. Does everyone realize it's after midnight?

KORIE: Sure, Jase. Hey, Willie, you should grill them some of those burgers you make.

JOHN LUKE: Yeah, I'm kind of hungry too.

BELLA, SADIE, AND WILL: Yeah, us too, Dad.

WILLIE: What? Oh, all right! Bring your group over, Jase. We'll continue the study over here with my midnight burgers!

The action moves back to center stage. Phil walks out holding his Bible to give the lesson.

PHIL: Our story today is based on the Parable of the Friend in Need told in Luke chapter 11. Let me read this story to you.

> *Suppose someone has a friend. He goes to him at midnight. He says, "Friend, lend me three loaves of bread. A friend of mine on a journey has come to stay with me. I have nothing for him to eat."*

Then the one inside answers, "Don't bother me. The door is already locked. My children are with me in bed. I can't get up and give you anything."

I tell you, that person will not get up. And he won't give the man bread just because he is his friend. But because the man keeps on asking, he will get up. He will give him as much as he needs.

So here is what I say to you. Ask, and it will be given to you. Search, and you will find. Knock, and the door will be opened to you. Everyone who asks will receive. He who searches will find. And the door will be opened to the one who knocks (Matthew 11:5 – 10).

Jesus told this parable to teach us an important lesson. A prayer is like a knock on God's door, and God will open that door when we keep knocking on it. He doesn't want us to give up if we don't get the answer right away. We need to be like Jase in our skit today. Jase needed help, and he knew where he could get that help. He understood that he just had to knock on Willie's door—and keep on knocking—and eventually that door would be opened to him. It's the same way with God. We have to be ravenous—or hungry like Jase and his friends at the Bible study—and keep on praying for the answer.

Now, Miss Kay and I have had a few visitors down at our house. Miss Kay can make some tasty biscuits, and I make some pretty tasty jelly. We also love to fry fish. When our neighbors know we're cooking, they come knocking at our door—and if they knock, we let them in. Sometimes we get tired of having company or hearing someone knocking on our door, but not God. He is always happy, happy, happy to have one of His children come to Him in prayer. So don't forget your prayers—before a meal, or before you go to bed, or when you wake up every morning. God will be waiting to hear from you.

Willie and the gang come out dressed like clowns, blowing duck calls.

WILLIE: See, I told y'all they were clowns! Well, what a great lesson we had today on seeking God through a life of ravenous prayer. Now it's time for y'all to get with your groups and head off to your breakout stations. Have a great time learning about how to seek God in prayer!

Duck calls blow and music plays as the kids head out to their stations.

CLOSING ROUNDUP

Have the music playing as the children return from their final station. Once everyone is back in the room, say a few words to wrap up the day's events, or have one of your group leaders (or the character dressed as Phil) do the recap. The following is a sample script that you can follow.

— SCRIPT —

So, did y'all have a great time at Willie's Redneck Rodeo today? *(The kids respond, "Yes!")* Great!

Okay, who here can tell me what it means to be "ravenous" in prayer? *(Let a few kids in the audience respond.)* That's right—it means to have an unquenchable hunger for talking and listening to God. It means to keep asking, seeking, and knocking on God's door and not give up when we pray. Now, does this mean that we will always get what we ask God to give us? *(Let a few kids in the audience respond.)* Nope. God will always give us what is best for us, but that doesn't mean it will always be what we want. Sometimes God may have to answer our prayers with a "no" or a "wait."

Our family ends each episode of *Duck Dynasty*® with a prayer. We do so because the Robertson family believes that prayer is essential in our walk with God. Many people have told us that they like this part of the show, and we're glad they do—but really this is just how we are. We always want to include God in our day, and praying to Him is just one way to include Him.

The Bible tells us in 1 Thessalonians 5:17 to "never stop praying." That means we should have a heart that is always open to God's Word and a mouth that is always willing to ask God to supply our needs. We can call on God to give us wisdom, strength, comfort, or anything else we need. God is good all the time, and He is always ready to listen and supply what His children need.

So, who here would like to share a short story of what you learned today about ravenous prayer, or about something you REALLY prayed for one time? *(Allow the children to share as time allows, or share a few personal stories of things you observed today or how you have been persistent in prayer in your life.)*

⎡— CLOSING PRAYER AND DISMISSAL —⎤

Thank the children who shared their stories with the group. Close by expressing your gratitude to God for giving us His Word, the Bible. Ask God to continue to help the children have hearts that are hungry to keep on seeking Him in prayer. The following is a sample you can use:

Dear God, help us to always come to You first when we need something. Help us to be persistent in prayer. Thank You for Your promise in the Bible that You hear our prayers and that we don't need to worry about anything. Please show us the people around us who are in need, and help us to remember to pray for them. We love You, God. In Jesus's name, Amen.

Tell the children that tomorrow's theme will be obedience, so they need to make sure they come back for more fun at Willie's Redneck Rodeo!

DAY FOUR
REAL OBEDIENCE

MAIN POINT: It takes real obedience for us to obey God and follow His commands!

MEMORY VERSE: 2 John 1:6

Preschool and Early Elementary: "The way we show our love is to obey God's commands."

Later Elementary: "The way we show our love is to obey God's commands. He commands you to lead a life of love."

BIBLE STORY: The Parable of the Two Sons (Matthew 21:28–32).

SUGGESTED SONGS: "You, You, You" from *Sky* VBS (Group Publishing); "I Believe in Jesus" from *Super Strong God* by Hillsong Kids (Hillsong)

OPENING ROUNDUP

As the children arrive and get settled into their groups, have your Rockin' Rednecks leading songs up front or some other worship and praise music playing in the background. At the scheduled start time, provide some opening remarks, remind the children about the ground rules for their behavior during the VBS, and encourage them to participate in all of the stations. Note that you will need a few additional props for this skit. After your opening comments, the actors will come on stage to perform it.

PROPS

- Several large plastic or rubber frogs
- Blunt knife (no sharp edges) to pretend to cut up the frogs

CHARACTERS AND COSTUMES

WILLIE (bandana, long hair, brown beard, plaid shirt)

JASE (black stocking cap and clothing, long brown hair, brown beard)

MISS KAY (shoulder-length black hair, apron)

PHIL (long gray beard, camo headband, camo clothes)

SI (camo cap, T-shirt, camo shirt, glasses, gray beard, carries plastic cup)

SCRIPT

Willie and Jase walk out to center stage and face the audience.

WILLIE: Hey, y'all. Are we ready to go "crazy redneck"?

JASE: I can go crazy redneck better than you.

WILLIE: What? I invented "crazy redneck"!

JASE: You think you are soooo good.

WILLIE: Is that a redneck challenge?

JASE: Yep! Dance off! Turn up the music! Yeeehaaaw!

WILLIE: It's on. Let's all sing!

The Rockin' Rednecks come out and lead a few worship songs (refer to Rockin' Rednecks suggested praise music at the beginning of Day 4).

WILLIE: It was me! I'm the winner.

JASE: Are you kidding? You have no moves.

Miss Kay walks out onto the stage.

MISS KAY: Boys! Boys! You two have to calm down.

WILLIE: Well ... he's the one who started it.

JASE: Really? How old are you?

MISS KAY *(turns to the audience)*: These boys have always been competitive. I heard yesterday that they were even challenging one another as to who could ride a buckin' bull the longest! Can you believe that? These boys were always a "challenge" as well when it came to obeying me and their dad. Hey, do you kids want to hear a story about Jase and Willie when they were growing up? *(Kids respond, "Yes!")*

Phil enters from the side and walks onto the stage.

PHIL: Miss Kay, before we get to the story about these two, let's take a moment to review. Now, each day this week we have been looking at a different parable that Jesus told. Who can remind me what a "parable" is? *(Let a few kids respond.)* Yes, it is an earthly story with a heavenly meaning. Now, let's all think waaaay back to the first day. Who can tell me what we learned about? Redonkulous ... *(Let a few kids respond.)* That's right—redonkulous faith. What did we learn on day two? Radical ... *(Let a few kids respond.)* Yes, radical forgiveness. And what did we talk about yesterday? Ravenous ... *(Let a few kids respond.)* You got it—ravenous prayer. God wants us to be hungry when we come to Him in prayer and keep on asking, seeking, and knocking at His door. Miss Kay, what are we going to be learning about today?

Phil will need to exit and circle behind the stage to the Duck Call Shop as Miss Kay talks.

MISS KAY: Today we are going to be learning about "real" obedience. Real obedience is a matter of the heart. Speaking of which, let's get back to that story about my two boys. You see, I love my boys, but there were times when they did not want to obey me.

Jase and Willie motion as if they can't believe Miss Kay would say such a thing. The action moves across the stage to the Duck Call Shop, where Phil and Si are cleaning some frogs after a big hunt. Phil is chopping them up as Si enjoys his tea. Jase walks over to the shop.

JASE: Hey, Phil, looks like y'all got some beauties here. How many frogs you get?

PHIL: 'Bout a dozen.

SI: Two dozen at least, Jack! Some of the biggest legs I've seen. You should've been there.

PHIL: He was off being a neighborhood yuppie.

JASE: I couldn't help it. I had to work on our flowerbeds.

SI: Isn't that what you have sons for?

PHIL: Jase, I need you to do something for me.

JASE: Actually, I have to go . . .

PHIL *(unfazed, keeps talking)*: I need you to go and pull up the boat we used to get these beauties and bring up our spotlight and gig.

JASE: I have to go, Dad. I was just coming out here to the shed to borrow your weed-eater.

SI: Weed-eater? Phil, I didn't know you had a weed-eater.

JASE: I gotta go, Dad. Really.

SI: I might need to borrow that weed-eater.

PHIL: Yuppie life.

Jase exits one side of the stage while Willie approaches from the other.

WILLIE: Hey, Phil! Miss Kay told me you and Si pulled in a bunch of frogs. When are we eatin' 'em?

PHIL: Hey, my boy, I have a job I need you to do.

WILLIE: Okay . . . sure, what do you need?

PHIL: I need you to go down to the river and check my nets. I'd go, but Si and I are busy cleaning these here frogs.

WILLIE: Sure . . . but it doesn't look like Si is really working.

SI: Are you kidding me? I'm encouraging Phil.

WILLIE: All right. I'll go do it right now.

PHIL: Good boy.

WILLIE: I'll be back when the frog legs are ready.

Phil and Si exit the stage. Willie walks from the Duck Call Shop over to center stage. Jase approaches center stage from the side and meets up with Willie.

WILLIE: Hey, man, I didn't know you were here. Did you see all those frogs Dad and Si caught?

JASE: Yeah, I saw 'em. I shouldn't even be here though. I need to be working on our flowerbeds. But ... Dad asked me to pull their boat in and get their spotlight and gig. At first I didn't really want to spend the time doing it, but I thought about it and decided it won't take toooo long. So I came back to get it done for Phil.

WILLIE: Well, Phil asked me to go check the nets at the river. But I think I'll do it later. See ya, man.

JASE: He gone.

Willie and Jase leave one side of the stage. Phil approaches from the other side holding his Bible to give the lesson.

PHIL: Our story today is based on the Parable of the Two Sons. Since I have four sons, I can kind of relate. This story is found in Matthew chapter 21, and it goes like this:

A man had two sons. He went to the first and said, "Son, go and work today in the vineyard."

"I will not," the son answered. But later he changed his mind and went. Then the father went to the other son. He said the same thing. The son answered, "I will, sir." But he did not go (Matthew 21:28–30).

When Jesus finished telling this story, He asked His listeners which of the two sons did what their father wanted. They correctly answered, "the first son." Like Jase in our skit today, that son had a bad attitude, but he eventually did what his father had asked. The second son—like Willie in our skit—had a good attitude and said yes to his dad right away. But he didn't follow through and obey.

Real obedience is all about doing what we are told to do even when we don't want to do it. Y'all may not know this, but I played football when I was in college. We had to practice every day, and there were plenty of days when I would have rather been out hunting than playing football. But I was raised to respect my teachers and my coaches, so I practiced even when I didn't feel like doing so. Over time, that practice paid off, and I discovered there were many good benefits from being obedient to my coaches.

When you're obedient to your parents, teachers, and coaches, you're also learning to be obedient to God. You never know what God might ask you to do, so you just have to be ready to be obedient. The Bible says in Jeremiah 29:11 that God knows the plans He has for you. You just have to be willing to go where He sends you and do what He asks you to do.

Willie and the gang come out blowing duck calls.

WILLIE: All right, kids. What a great lesson we had today on the importance of being obedient. Now it's time to go to our breakout classes and learn more about how we can practice real obedience to God!

Duck calls blow and music plays as the kids head out to their stations.

CLOSING ROUNDUP

Have the music playing as the children return from their final station. Once everyone is back in the room, say a few words to wrap up the day's events, or have one of your group leaders (or the character dressed as Phil) do the recap. The following is a sample script that you can follow.

— SCRIPT —

Did y'all have a great time at Willie's Redneck Rodeo today? *(The kids respond, "Yes!")* All right!

So, now that y'all have been to your stations today, who can tell me what "real obedience" means? *(Let a few kids in the audience respond.)* Yes, it means to be obedient to God even when it's not easy to do so. It means to obey those who are in authority over you. When I say "authority," that just means someone who is like a "boss" to you. That would be your parents, and it could also be a coach, a teacher, a babysitter, or an older brother or sister. It doesn't mean that you just obey what *anyone* says to you, because there will be times when your friends will want you to do something that you know you shouldn't do. God has the most authority in your life. That is why it is important to know what the Bible says—so you always know what you should and shouldn't do.

Now, in Ephesians 6:1, we read, "Children, obey your parents as believers in the Lord. Obey them because it's the right thing to do." The Bible makes it very clear that children are to obey their parents. However, many times parents have to ask their children again and again to do a certain thing. That is not *real* obedience! Real obedience is obeying your parents the first time they ask you to do something. Now, did you know that God makes a promise to you when you choose to obey your mom and dad? He does! Ephesians 6:2–3 states, " 'Honor your father and mother.' That is the first commandment that has a promise. 'Then things will go well with you. You will live a long time on the earth.' "

Just think about that promise for a minute. Y'all can probably remember times in your life when things went well for you when you chose to obey your folks. I know that was true for the oldest Robertson boy, Alan. When he was a teenager, he decided to disobey his parents and did things he shouldn't do. He left his family and tried to live his life without his parents or God. Life was hard for Alan for a while, but soon he realized that his parents loved him and wanted the best for him. Eventually Alan returned home.

So, who here would like to share a short story of what you learned today about real obedience, or when something worked out REALLY well for you when you decided to obey your parents? *(Allow the children to share as time allows, or share a few personal stories of things you observed today or how you have had to learn obedience in your life.)*

CLOSING PRAYER AND DISMISSAL

Thank the children who shared their stories with the group. Close by expressing your gratitude to God for giving us His Word, the Bible. Ask God to continue to help the children have hearts that are always seeking to honor God by obeying Him. The following is a sample prayer you can use:

Dear God, thank You so much for giving us examples about real obedience in the Bible. Help us to obey You, our parents, our teachers, and other adults who want to help us. Help us to be open to Your direction so we can know what You want us to do. We love You, God. In Jesus's name, Amen.

Tell the children that tomorrow will be the final day of Willie's Redneck Rodeo. The theme will be kindness, so they need to make sure they come back for more fun!

DAY FIVE ROWDY KINDNESS

MAIN POINT: God wants us to be loud and rowdy when it comes to being kind to others!

MEMORY VERSE: Colossians 3:12

> *Preschool and Early Elementary:* "Put on tender mercy and kindness as if they were your clothes."

> *Later Elementary:* "You are God's chosen people. You are holy and dearly loved. So put on tender mercy and kindness as if they were your clothes. Don't be proud. Be gentle and patient."

BIBLE STORY: The Parable of the Good Samaritan (Luke 10:25–37).

SUGGESTED SONGS: "Live It Out" from *Big Apple Adventure* VBS by Jeff Slaughter (LifeWay Music); "Every Move I Make" from *Great Worship Songs for Kids*, vol. 1 (Brentwood Benson).

OPENING ROUNDUP

As the children arrive and get settled into their groups, have your Rockin' Rednecks leading songs up front or some other worship and praise music playing in the background. At the scheduled start time, provide some opening remarks, remind the children about the ground rules for their behavior during the VBS, and encourage them to participate in all of the stations. After your opening comments, the actors will come on stage to perform the skit. For today's scene, you will need to move some of the chairs from the Duck Call Shop closer to the audience to serve as an "outdoor" location. You will also need a volunteer to play a cell phone ring (or make a noise like one).

PROPS

- A large cardboard box
- Several coffee cups
- A binder or photo album (place inside the box)
- A cellphone (for Willie)

CHARACTERS AND COSTUMES

SI (camo cap, T-shirt, camo shirt, glasses, gray beard, carries plastic cup)

JASE (black stocking cap and clothing, long brown hair, brown beard)

PHIL (long gray beard, camo headband, camo clothes)

MISS KAY (shoulder-length black hair, camo scarf or apron)

WILLIE (bandana, long hair, brown beard, plaid shirt)

KORIE (long blond hair)

SCRIPT

Si and Jase walk out to center stage and face the audience.

SI: Hey, Jack! Y'all ready to get rowdy? (*Kids respond, "Yay!"*) Hey, hey, you call that rowdy? I mean like ROWDY, JACK! (*Si starts jumping and dancing around.*)

JASE (looking perplexed): Si? What are you doin'?

SI: Come on, Jase! We gettin' rowdy in here ... let's all sing!

The Rockin' Rednecks come out and lead a few worship songs (refer to Rockin' Rednecks suggested praise music at the beginning of Day 5).

JASE: SI! Why are you going crazy and dancin'? You're gonna shake something loose.

SI: Our lesson today is about gettin' *ROWDY!* I got this!

JASE: SI! Our lesson today is about rowdy *kindness*!

SI *(stops dancing)*: Kindness? Rowdy ... kindness?

JASE: Yeah. It means to be *loud* about being kind!

SI: Oh, like *(hollering)*, HEY, JASE! WOULD YOU LIKE ME TO GET YOU SOME TEA?

JASE: Si! No ... not talkin' LOUD. It's about being LOUD in the way we treat others with kindness. In most things in life being rowdy might not be appreciated—like your dancin'—but when it comes to being kind, we need to be loud on purpose.

SI: Hmmm ... maybe we should share a story with the kids about this today.

Phil walks out on center stage.

PHIL: Now hold up, Si! This is our last day at Willie's Redneck Rodeo, so I want to make sure all the kids remember what they've learned this week. *(Turns to audience.)* Okay, y'all ready to review? Who here remembers what we call the stories that Jesus told in the Bible? *(Let the kids respond.)* Yes, they are called "parables." Jesus told these simple stories about everyday life to help the people understand more about God. Now, let's go waaaay back to day one. On that day we learned about redonkulous ... *(Let a few kids respond.)* You got it—redonkulous faith. On day two we learned about radical ... *(Let a few kids respond.)* Yes, radical forgiveness. On day three we talked about ravenous ... *(Let a few kids respond.)* Right again—ravenous prayer. And yesterday we talked about real ... *(Let a few kids respond.)* Y'all are good. Real obedience. That's the type of obedience where we do what our parents say even when it's not easy.

SI: Whew, that's a lot! Well, I'm ready. But where's my tea? Jase, did you steal my cup?

JASE: Pipe down, Si! You and Phil need to head over to the Duck Call Shop now, 'cause you're both in the story I'm about to tell.

Phil and Si walk over to the Duck Call Shop and sit down in the chairs. They pick up their coffee cups and start sipping from them.

JASE: Now, our story today takes us out to the front yard of Phil and Miss Kay's house . . .

Jase exits the stage while Miss Kay enters from the other side carrying the large box. She approaches Si and Phil sitting in the chairs.

MISS KAY: Good morning, fellas!

PHIL: Miss Kay, let me get that box for ya.

SI: Yeah . . . Phil needs to be carrying that, not you.

MISS KAY: Why, thank you, fellas.

PHIL: Miss Kay, what are you up to with this box?

MISS KAY: Weeelll, I was hopin' that you would ask . . . cuz I am headed to the storeroom. I need to sort through a few things in this box, and maybe pick out some things from the storeroom. I'm having my muffin group ladies here in a few days, and I just know I have the perfect decorations. It will just take a little time to find them all.

As Miss Kay continues to talk, Phil slowly sets down the box. He and Si begin to sneak away.

MISS KAY: Do you remember those cute little . . . *(she looks around).* Phil? Si? Fellas? *(She looks over and sees Phil and Si still sneaking away.)* Now where are you two going?

PHIL *(over his shoulder)***:** Uh, gotta go, Miss Kay!

SI: Yeah! We heard them beavers buildin' a dam!

MISS KAY: Ooookay! Bring me back some squirrels, ya hear? *(Turns to the kids.)* I think those fellas just didn't wanna help me. *(She picks up the box and carries it to the desk in the Duck Call Shop. She opens the box.)* Hmmm . . . I just know those decorations are somewhere. Oh, look at this! *(She takes out the album.)* A photo album! My boys are soooo cute. That Willie has some dimples, but just look how cute my Jep is! What a precious baby!

Jase and Willie walk out onto the stage.

WILLIE: Hey, Jase, what is Kay doing?

JASE: Oh . . . this looks like trouble. She is in the storeroom.

WILLIE: Nah, let's go check it out. Maybe she has some food in there.

JASE: Is that all you think about? Man, beware! We are fixin' to get sucked into a job.

WILLIE: Relax. I got this.

Willie and Jase approach Miss Kay in the storeroom.

JASE: Hey, Mom. What are you doing?

WILLIE: You got any food?

MISS KAY: Heyyyy ... it's two of my favorite sons!

JASE *(to Willie)*: Trouble!

WILLIE *(to Jase)*: I said relax! I got this.

MISS KAY: Hey, you boys can help me. Do you remember those cute decorations I used the time we had all the family over and I cooked my special muffins? Weeelll, I am having my ladies' group over here to the house, and I'd like to use them again. But I just can't remember where I put them. I'm sure they are in here somewhere. You remember, don't you? They would be just perfect for my table decorations.

JASE *(making an alarm sound)*: Beep, beep, beep! Mayday! Mayday!

The volunteer offstage will need to play the cellphone ring tone at this point (or mimic one).

WILLIE: Hold on, Kay, I'm getting a phone call.

JASE *(rolling his eyes)*: How convenient.

MISS KAY: I see. Well then, Jase, could you please get me those boxes wayyyy back in the corner? That has to be where I put those decorations. Don't you remember how cute they were?

JASE: Oh, yes, I remember how *cute* they were. Willie! Hurry up!

WILLIE *(talking into the phone)*: What do you need? You say there's trouble at the warehouse ... and you need me to come to help you *right now. (Pauses.)* Okay, got it. Sure ... I'll be right there. *(Puts away the phone and speaks to Jase.)* Jase, we gotta go! The warehouse just called, and they need us.

JASE: Sorry, Miss Kay ... I gotta go with Willie.

MISS KAY: That's okay, boys, go make some more duck calls. I'll just keep looking for those decorations myself. I just know they will be perfect for my party.

Willie and Jase walk to center stage, out of earshot of Miss Kay.

JASE: So, they need us at the warehouse?

WILLIE: No! I just talked to Jep and the fish are bitin'!

The boys sneak out while Miss Kay continues to look around the storeroom and in the box.

MISS KAY: Whew, I'm tired. It sure is hot out here!

Korie enters and approaches Miss Kay.

KORIE: Hey, Miss Kay! You sure look tired.

MISS KAY: I am! Say, do you remember those cute decorations I had that time the family came over? I'm having my muffin ladies over at the house, and I want it to be special.

KORIE: Well, a little birdie told me you had a special event coming up, so I brought you some of my decorations to use.

MISS KAY: Oh, I LOVE them! They're perfect.

KORIE: Oh, Miss Kay, your decorations are always perfect. You know just how to put the finishing touches on a meaningful evening. Do you want me to help you find your other decorations?

MISS KAY: No, let's go in and make the men some food. I know they all left to get out of helping me today, but they'll be back, especially when they get hungry. Let's make them something special and kill 'em with kindness.

KORIE: Or maybe give 'em a little sweet indigestion!

Korie and Miss Kay exit the stage. Phil walks out holding his Bible to give the lesson.

PHIL: This story today, my little brothers and sisters, reminds me of a familiar parable in the Bible. It's called the Parable of the Good Samaritan, and you can find it in Luke chapter 10. Let's read a little of that story.

One day an authority on the law stood up to put Jesus to the test. "Teacher," he asked, "what must I do to receive eternal life?"

"What is written in the Law?" Jesus replied. "How do you understand it?"

He answered, " 'Love the Lord your God with all your heart and with all your soul. Love him with all your strength and with all your mind.' And, 'Love your neighbor as you love yourself.' "

"You have answered correctly," Jesus replied. "Do that, and you will live."

But the man wanted to make himself look good. So he asked Jesus, "And who is my neighbor?"

Jesus replied, "A man was going down from Jerusalem to Jericho. Robbers attacked him. They stripped off his clothes and beat him. Then they went away, leaving him almost dead. A priest happened to be going down that same road. When he saw the man, he passed by on the other side. A Levite also came by. When he saw the man, he passed by on the other side too.

But a Samaritan came to the place where the man was. When he saw the man, he felt sorry for him. He went to him, poured olive oil and wine on his wounds and bandaged them. Then he put the man on his own donkey. He took him to an inn and took care of him. The next day he took out two silver coins. He gave them to the owner of the inn. 'Take care of him,' he said. 'When I return, I will pay you back for any extra expense you may have.'

"Which of the three do you think was a neighbor to the man who was attacked by robbers?"

The authority on the law replied, "The one who felt sorry for him."

Jesus told him, "Go and do as he did" (Luke 10:25 – 37).

Jesus told this parable to teach us an important lesson about how we are to treat one another. Now, in our skit today, me and Uncle Si weren't too kind to Miss Kay. We were kind of like the priest in this parable who passed by on the other side of the road. Jase and Willie weren't too kind to Miss Kay either. They were kind of like the Levite in Jesus's story. But then Korie arrived and gave Miss Kay some of her own decorations. She was kind of like the Good Samaritan in this story, cause she took the time to help. Jesus says this is how we should be—we need to show rowdy kindness to one another!

I know it's not always easy to treat your friends or even your brothers and sisters with kindness, but God says this is the best way to live. Now that I'm older, I can see this. Since our TV show has become popular, there are some people who have started to talk mean about us. But I tell them I love them—and I let it go at that. It never does any good to be mean back. A lot of being kind is saying the right thing when the wrong thing happens. But first, this begins in your heart. You have to change your heart in order to say and do kind things. Hey, if this old guy can do it, you can too!

Willie and the gang come out blowing duck calls.

WILLIE: All right, kids, we just had another great lesson about how we should treat others with out-loud-and-on-purpose kindness. Now it's time to go have fun with some of my favorite people on our last day of Willie's Redneck Rodeo. So let's go out and get *ROWDY* for Jesus!

Duck calls blow and music plays as the kids head out to their stations.

CLOSING ROUNDUP

Have the music playing as the children return from their final station. Once everyone is back in the room, say a few words to wrap up the kids' time this week at Willie's Redneck Rodeo. Have one of your group leaders (or the character dressed as Phil) do the recap. Also, have each of your actors on hand to do one final "curtain call" for the kids. The following is a sample script that you can follow.

SCRIPT

Hey, kids, today is the last day of Willie's Redneck Rodeo. Did y'all have a great time this week at VBS? *(The kids respond, "Yes!")*

So, now that y'all have been to your stations today, who can tell me what "rowdy kindness" means? *(Let a few kids in the audience respond.)* I can see you paid attention today. Rowdy kindness means to be LOUD about being kind. In most things in life being rowdy might not be appreciated, but when it comes to being kind to others, it's great to be out loud on purpose!

In our parable today, a man was beaten up by robbers and left on the side of a road, and three people came by afterward. The first two travelers passed right on by, but the third traveler showed him kindness. Now, what's amazing about this third traveler was that he was a Samaritan, which means he was practically the injured man's *enemy*. It couldn't have been easy for him to show kindness, but he did it anyway. That's rowdy kindness.

Being rowdy about kindness means to choose to treat everyone you meet with a kind and respectful spirit. It means looking for ways that you can make a difference in the lives of others and treating them kindly and respectfully. Now, you won't always receive this same behavior from others. In today's world, bullying is a problem at school, on the playground, and on the Internet. But bullying is not how God wants you to act toward others. He wants you to see others the way He sees them. You have to forget about being wronged and accept God's desire for you to be kind no matter what.

This will be hard to do sometimes. One time when Phil was going to be on another TV show, a man got mad at him and his family and starting calling them names. But all Phil said was, "I love him anyway." Phil understood that God asked him to treat others with kindness, and nothing was going to stop him from doing that. So, what about you? Who would like to share a short story of what you learned today about rowdy kindness, or about how you were kind to someone when it was REALLY difficult to do so? *(Allow the children to share as time allows, or share a few personal stories of things you observed today or how you have practiced rowdy kindness in your life.)*

All right! Thank you for everyone who shared. Well, the Robertsons sure enjoyed having you all spend time with them this week. So let's bring them out one last time and give them a big round of applause. *(Announce each of your actors: Martin, Godwin, Mountain Man, Bella, John Luke, Sadie, Will, Jep, Jase, Korie, Miss Kay, Si, Willie, Phil.)*

CLOSING PRAYER AND DISMISSAL

Close by expressing your gratitude to God for giving us His Word, the Bible. Ask God to bless the children for the time they spent at Willie's Redneck Rodeo this week, and ask Him to help them put everything they have learned into practice. The following is a sample prayer you can use:

Dear God, thank You for bringing each person here this week to learn more about You and Your Word, the Bible. Thank You for everything You have taught us. Thank You for being kind and loving to us. Now, we ask that You please help us to have a heart of kindness to everyone we meet. We want to be kind just like You! Help us to remember to put everything we learned into practice so we can continue to be more like You. We love You, God. In Jesus's name, Amen.

Thank the children one last time for spending the week with you at VBS. Blow the duck calls one more time and close your time together.

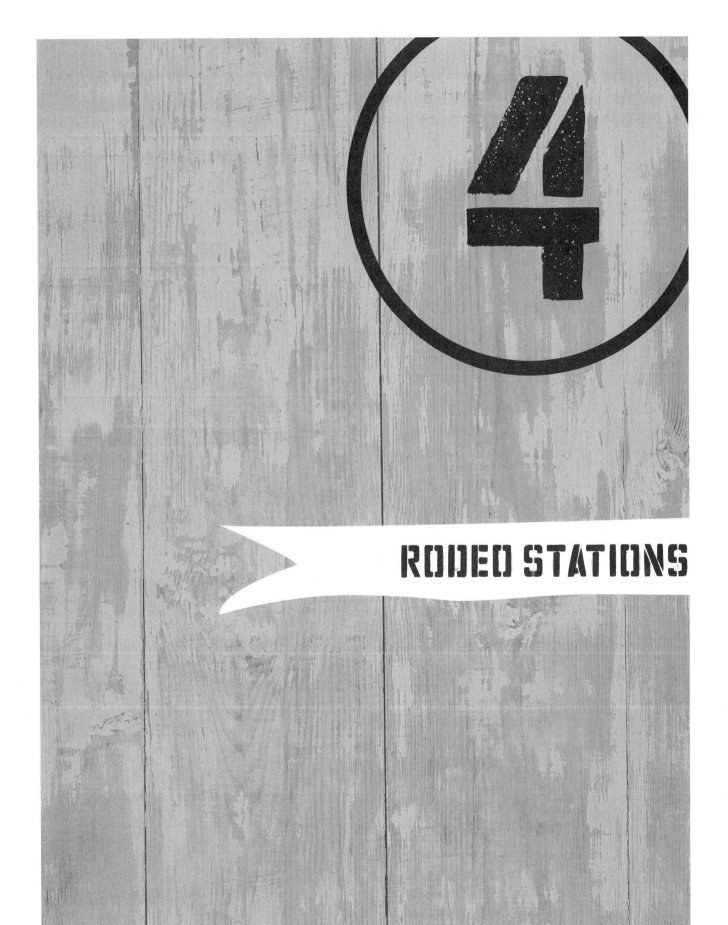

4

RODEO STATIONS

MISSY'S MUSIC AND MEMORY

Missy loves to sing—in fact, she comes from a whole family of singers—and your kids will also enjoy this time of music and Scripture memorization. Worshiping God through interactive songs is a powerful way to help children hide the truth of Scripture in their hearts, and the activities they will do during this time will help them to really cement the day's Scripture verse in their heads. Don't be concerned if your gift isn't being a song leader, as there are many great tracks with vocals that you can use so that your group can "sing along" with the kids on the song. During this rotation your children will be doing both memory work and music, so decide ahead of time how much time you will spend on each activity. Also note that two sets of memory verses have been provided for you to use based on the ages of your group members.

MISSY'S MUSIC AND MEMORY STATION ROTATION SCHEDULE

TIME	GROUP 1	GROUP 2	GROUP 3	GROUP 4	GROUP 5
9:00–9:25 am 5:30–5:55 pm	Opening Roundup	Opening Roundup	Opening Roundup	Opening Roundup	Opening Roundup
9:30–9:55 am 6:00–6:25 pm	Missy's Music and Memory	Si's Bull Pen	Miss Kay's Kitchen	The Warehouse	Korie's Craft Shed
10:00–10:25 am 6:30–6:55 pm	Korie's Craft Shed	Missy's Music and Memory	Si's Bull Pen	Miss Kay's Kitchen	The Warehouse
10:30–10:55 am 7:00–7:25 pm	The Warehouse	Korie's Craft Shed	Missy's Music and Memory	Si's Bull Pen	Miss Kay's Kitchen
11:00–11:25 am 7:30–7:55 pm	Miss Kay's Kitchen	The Warehouse	Korie's Craft Shed	Missy's Music and Memory	Si's Bull Pen
11:30–11:55 am 8:00–8:25 pm	Si's Bull Pen	Miss Kay's Kitchen	The Warehouse	Korie's Craft Shed	Missy's Music and Memory
12:00–12:15 pm 8:30–8:45 pm	Closing Roundup	Closing Roundup	Closing Roundup	Closing Roundup	Closing Roundup

SETTING UP THE STATION

A choir or music room in your church would serve as a perfect location for this 20-minute rotation, though any other room would also work as long as the children are not disturbing other groups. To make this Missy's Music Room, print out pictures of Missy (either full color or gray scale; see DVD-ROM) and post them in various places around the site. Consider purchasing large foam squares that lock together for the children to sit on, or you can just have the kids grab a mat and sit down. Having these foam squares or mats will give the children freedom to jump around and move in a small area without knocking into chairs. It can also help when you need to call the kids to attention and get them to settle down. For example, you can say, "Okay, now it's time to work on your memory verses. Everyone needs to find their square and sit down on it."

Make sure you set up the electronic equipment you will need ahead of time to meet your needs. Take time to prepare your music selections so that you can move from one song to the next quickly and easily. The songs suggested for each day are available on iTunes or other sites, so consider downloading the music to your iPhone or another device that will allow you to plug right into your sound system. In this way, your music will be readily available as the children come in to the room. Early preparation will really keep the energy and focus of your time together on track.

For the memory work, remember that the younger kids will have an easier time with memorization if you include hand motions. These do not need to be complicated—simple

is good. Some sample suggestions have been included for each day, but feel free to make up your own (or have your students help you). The activity listed for each day has also been designed to help your group members retain the memory verse. Don't underestimate the importance of this time, for when kids can hide God's Word in their hearts, it serves as a compass to guide them and enables them to stay strong in their faith when crises and trouble come their way.

DAY ONE: REDONKULOUS FAITH

MAIN IDEA

Following God requires a "redonkulous" amount of faith!

SUGGESTED SONGS

1. "By Faith" from *Under God* by Jeff Slaughter (Indie Music)
2. "Faith" from *Sing 'Em Again: Favorite VBS Songs for Families*, vol. 3 (Group Publishing)
3. "We Can Trust Him (Psalm 33:4)" from *Sing 'Em Again: Favorite VBS Songs for Families*, vol. 5 (Group Publishing)
4. "King of the Jungle" from *Great Worship Songs for Kids*, vol. 1 (Brentwood Benson)
5. "The One True God" from *Sing 'Em Again: Favorite Holy Land VBS Songs for Families*, vol. 2 (Group Publishing)

MEMORY VERSE
1 CORINTHIANS 16:13

Preschool and Early Elementary: "Be on your guard. Stand firm in the faith."

Later Elementary: "Be on your guard. Stand firm in the faith. Be brave. Be strong."

SAMPLE MOTIONS FOR YOUNGER CHILDREN

When you say the word "be," put your fingers on the side of your head like a bee's antennae. Point to yourself when you say "you," and then salute when you say "guard." Stand at attention when you say "stand firm," and close your eyes and fold your hands when you say "faith."

MEMORY GAME
PASS THE BALL

For this game, you will need a dry-erase board, markers, and a small ball. Write the memory verse on the board and go over it several times before the game begins. Erase one word at a time and have children continue to repeat the verse until all the words are gone. Next, have the children stand in a circle and place them side by side, boy-girl-boy-girl. Start the music and have the children "pass" a ball around the circle (remind them to pass—*not throw*—the ball). When the music stops, the child with the ball will get to say the verse. Continue until everyone has had an opportunity to say the verse on his or her own. (For the older groups, have a competition between the boys and girls. If one team misses the word, the other team gets the chance to answer. Keep

score, and declare the team with the most points at the end to be the winner.)

DAY TWO: RADICAL FORGIVENESS

MAIN IDEA

God wants us to forgive others in a radical way!

SUGGESTED SONGS

1. "His Great Love" from *Pandamania* VBS (Group Publishing)
2. "Revelation Song" from *Great Worship Songs for Kids*, vol. 5 (Brentwood Benson)
3. "East to West" by Casting Crowns on the album *The Altar and the Door* (Beach Street)
4. "Do to Others (Matthew 7:12)" from *God's Word in My Heart: Scripture Songs for Families (Matthew)* (Group Publishing)
5. "Give as Freely (Matthew 10:8)" from *God's Word in My Heart: Scripture Songs for Families (Matthew)* (Group Publishing)

MEMORY VERSE
COLOSSIANS 3:13

Preschool and Early Elementary: "Forgive, just as the Lord forgave you."

Later Elementary: "Put up with each other. Forgive the things you are holding against one another. Forgive, just as the Lord forgave you."

SAMPLE MOTIONS FOR YOUNGER CHILDREN

When you say the word "forgive," put your hands together like you're shaking your own hands. When you said "as the Lord," point to the sky. Join your hands back together for "forgave," and then point to yourself for the last word, "you."

MEMORY GAME
GOD'S TREASURE

For this game, you will need a box with a lid (a shoebox will work) and candy or other prizes (place inside the box). Have the children sit in a circle, go over the memory verse four or five times, and then ask the children to pass the box around the circle. Each child will need to say the next word of the memory verse as they are passing the box. The child holding the box at the end of the verse gets to open the box, take a treat, and then return to his or her seat. Repeat until all of the children have received a prize.

DAY THREE: RAVENOUS PRAYER

MAIN IDEA

God tells us in the Bible that we are to be persistent—or "ravenous"—in prayer!

SUGGESTED SONGS

1. "Watching Over You" from *Favorite VBS Songs for Families* (Group Publishing)
2. "Great Big God" from *Great Big God* (Kids Vineyard Worship UK).
3. "Rejoice in the Lord Always (Philippians 4:4)" from *God's Word in My Heart: Scripture Songs for Families (Thankful Times)* (Group Publishing)
4. "Ask (and It Will Be Given)" from *More Sing-a-Long Scripture Songs* (Great Worship Songs)
5. "Keep On (Matthew 7:7)" from *God's Word in My Heart: Scripture Songs for Families (Matthew)* (Group Music)
6. "Love and Pray (Matthew 5:44)" from *God's Word in My Heart: Scripture Songs for Families (Matthew)* (Group Publishing)

MEMORY VERSE
PHILIPPIANS 4:6

Preschool and Early Elementary: "Tell God about everything. Ask and pray. Give thanks to him."

Later Elementary: "Don't worry about anything. Instead, tell God about everything. Ask and pray. Give thanks to him."

SAMPLE MOTIONS FOR YOUNGER CHILDREN

When you say the word "God," point to the sky. When you say "everything," point your fingers all around the room. Move your hand like a mouth talking when you say "ask," and fold your hands together for "pray." Pat your shoulder for "give thanks."

MEMORY GAME
KING OF THE MOUNTAIN

For this game, you will need a short stepping stool or study chair. Go over the memory verse four or five times with the children. Choose one student to come to the front and try to say the memory verse. (Depending on the child's age, you might want to do the motions with him or her). Tell the child it is important to get the verse exactly correct, as the other students will be listening if he or she misses a word. (This will help the students who are listening to also learn the verse.) If the student gets the verse correct, he or she gets to step up on the stool and be King of the Mountain. The child can remain there until another student says the verse correctly, at which point that child steps up on the stool and becomes King. Play until you have lots of Kings!

DAY FOUR: REAL OBEDIENCE

MAIN IDEA

It takes real obedience for us to obey God and follow His commands!

SUGGESTED SONGS

1. "You, You, You" from *Sky* VBS (Group Publishing)
2. "I Believe in Jesus" from *Super Strong God* by Hillsong Kids (Hillsong)
3. "Obey My Commandments" from *God's Word in My Heart: Scripture Songs for Families (John)* (Group Publishing)
4. "The Lord's Plans" from *Sing 'Em Again: Favorite Holy Land VBS Songs for Families*, vol. 2 (Group Music)
5. "Trust in the Lord (Proverbs 3:5−6)" from *More Sing-a-Long Scripture Songs* (Great Worship Songs)

MEMORY VERSE
2 JOHN 1:6

Preschool and Early Elementary: "The way we show our love is to obey God's commands."

Later Elementary: "The way we show our love is to obey God's commands. He commands you to lead a life of love."

SAMPLE MOTIONS FOR YOUNGER CHILDREN

When you say the word "way," move your hand back and forth as if you are indicating a path. Put your hands out when you say "show," and cross them over your heart when you say "our love." Finally, put your hands together to make a book and open it when you say, "obey God's commands."

MEMORY GAME
CONCENTRATE!

For this game, you will need construction paper, card stock, or index cards. Ahead of time, write one word from the memory verse on each piece of paper, or write a few words from the verse on each sheet. (For example, "The way ... we show our ... love is ... to obey ... God's commands.") Next, create an identical second set so that the sheets create a matching pair. Keeping the sets separate, place the sheets face down and mix them up. When the memory time begins, divide the class into two teams. Explain that this game is similar to Concentration, but instead of finding matching pairs, they will be finding the correct order of the words in the memory verse. They can work together, alone, or as teams. At your discretion, they can use Bibles. If the competition gets too heated at any time, remind them they still need to "walk in love."

DAY FIVE: ROWDY KINDNESS

MAIN IDEA

God wants us to be loud and rowdy when it comes to being kind to others!

SUGGESTED SONGS

1. "Live It Out" from *Big Apple Adventure* VBS by Jeff Slaughter (LifeWay Music)
2. "Every Move I Make" from *Great Worship Songs for Kids*, vol. 1 (Brentwood Benson).
3. "How Can I Keep from Singing" from *Great Worship Songs for Kids*, vol. 2 (Brentwood Benson)
4. "Hands and Feet" from *Great Worship Songs for Kids*, vol. 2 (Brentwood Benson)
5. "Let Your Light Shine (Matthew 5:16)" from *God's Word in My Heart: Scripture Songs for Families (Matthew)* (Group Publishing)

MEMORY VERSE
COLOSSIANS 3:12

Preschool and Early Elementary: "Put on tender mercy and kindness as if they were your clothes."

Later Elementary: "You are God's chosen people. You are holy and dearly loved. So put on tender mercy and kindness as if they were your clothes. Don't be proud. Be gentle and patient."

SAMPLE MOTIONS FOR YOUNGER CHILDREN

Pretend that you are putting on a coat when you say "put on." When you say "tender mercy," throw your hands up in surrender. Make a wide smile and point to it when you say "kindness." Pat your shirt when you say "were your clothes."

MEMORY GAME
ROWDY KINDNESS PUZZLE

For this activity, you will need to print out the following sheet on card stock. Color in the words and the heart and cut it out to make a puzzle, or let the children color them during the memory time and create their own puzzles. When they are finished, have them recite the verse that they have put together.

ROWDY KINDNESS

INSTRUCTIONS: Color and cut out the puzzle, then rework.

Colossians 3:12 You are God's chosen people. You are holy and dearly loved. So put on tender mercy and kindness as if they were your clothes. Don't be proud. Be gentle and patient.

ROWDY KINDNESS

INSTRUCTIONS: Color and cut out the puzzle, then rework.

*Put on tender mercy and kindness
as if they were your clothes.*

Colossians 3:12

KORIE'S CRAFT SHED

Korie majored in Art Education in college, and she used her skills for many years at a Christian youth camp to teach the kids how to do various projects during their craft rotation. For this station in Willie's Redneck Rodeo, you will be able to create this same type of atmosphere as you guide your children in discovering their talents and allow them to let their creativity reign! Once again, you do not need to be concerned if you are not "artistic" in nature, for the crafts will be simple for the kids to put together, and they will have a lot of fun in just creating the projects. Remind them to always do their best, wash their brushes out when they change paint colors, and put their name on their work *before* they begin. Note that some options for each day's crafts have been provided, but you are free to direct your groups in any way you desire.

KORIE'S CRAFT SHED ROTATION SCHEDULE

TIME	GROUP 1	GROUP 2	GROUP 3	GROUP 4	GROUP 5
9:00–9:25 am 5:30–5:55 pm	Opening Roundup	Opening Roundup	Opening Roundup	Opening Roundup	Opening Roundup
9:30–9:55 am 6:00–6:25 pm	Missy's Music and Memory	Si's Bull Pen	Miss Kay's Kitchen	The Warehouse	Korie's Craft Shed
10:00–10:25 am 6:30–6:55 pm	Korie's Craft Shed	Missy's Music and Memory	Si's Bull Pen	Miss Kay's Kitchen	The Warehouse
10:30–10:55 am 7:00–7:25 pm	The Warehouse	Korie's Craft Shed	Missy's Music and Memory	Si's Bull Pen	Miss Kay's Kitchen
11:00–11:25 am 7:30–7:55 pm	Miss Kay's Kitchen	The Warehouse	Korie's Craft Shed	Missy's Music and Memory	Si's Bull Pen
11:30–11:55 am 8:00–8:25 pm	Si's Bull Pen	Miss Kay's Kitchen	The Warehouse	Korie's Craft Shed	Missy's Music and Memory
12:00–12:15 pm 8:30–8:45 pm	Closing Roundup	Closing Roundup	Closing Roundup	Closing Roundup	Closing Roundup

SETTING UP THE STATION

Your craft shed needs to be a room equipped with tables and chairs so the children will have plenty of room to explore their artistic skills. If possible, also choose a room with a sink. If you are concerned about spills, cover the tabletops with plastic tablecloths and tape them underneath to keep them from sliding off. You might also want to cover carpets and any other area that you want to keep paint-free with large plastic tarps. Purchasing painting smocks for each child in the group might be a good additional step to take to keep them from getting paint on their clothing. To make the station look like Korie's Craft Shed, print out pictures of Korie (either full-color or gray-scale; see DVD-ROM) and post them in various places around the site. Bring in props such as flowerpots, hammers, shovels, and pieces of wood to give the station a more authentic feel.

MASTER SUPPLIES LIST

Here is a complete list of the supplies that you will need to do each of the craft projects described in the next section:

- Large bottles of tempera paint in various colors
- Egg cartons for dividing the paint (cut the cartons in half and squeeze a different color into each of the six holes—two to four students can share each half-carton)
- Paintbrushes (at least one for each child)
- Jars or small plastic cups of water (so the children can rinse out their paintbrushes)
- Coffee filters (enough for two to three for each child)

- Green pipe cleaners
- Glue, paste, or tape
- Small white or brown paper bags
- Markers
- Child-safe scissors
- Yarn
- Small notebooks
- Colored duct tape (especially camouflage)
- Assorted stickers
- White paper plates (9-inch)
- Large roll of mural-sized paper
- Paper towels (to clean up any messes)

Always be sure to remind the children to do their best, to wash their brushes out when they change colors, and to put their names on their work *before* they begin.

DAY ONE: REDONKULOUS FAITH

MAIN IDEA

Our faith grows as we study God's Word and look at His creation.

SUPPLIES NEEDED

- Coffee filters
- Paint (note that this will work best with watered-down paint that absorbs easily into the filters and dries quickly)
- Green pipe cleaners
- Tape and/or glue

CRAFT
COFFEE FILTER FLOWERS

Give each child two to three coffee filters and ask the group members to paint them. When the children are finished, have them stack the coffee filters together to form the petals on a flower. If the filters do not stick together from the paint, have them glue the layers together. Next, give the group members a green pipe cleaner to serve as the stem. (If needed, give them additional pipe cleaners to support the petals and have them wind the cleaners together.) Make a loop at the top of the pipe cleaner and have the children glue or tape it to the back of the coffee filters. Close by reminding the group that our faith grows when we study God's Word and look at the wonders of creation!

DAY TWO: RADICAL FORGIVENESS

MAIN IDEA

God wants us to forgive others no matter who they are or what they have done.

SUPPLIES NEEDED

- Small white or brown paper bags
- Paint or markers
- Yarn (to create puppets' hair)

CRAFT
UNMERCIFUL SERVANT PUPPETS

Give each child a white or brown paper sack. Ask them to use the paint or markers to create one of the characters in the Parable of the Unmerciful Servant (the king, the unmerciful servant, the other servant). They can also paint a sack puppet of themselves if they prefer. Cut some strands of yarn and allow the kids to use it for the puppets' hair. When they are finished, read the Parable of the Unmerciful Servant from Matthew 19:21 – 35 and have them act out the story using their sack puppets. Close your time by reminding the group that God wants us to be like the king in the story and be radical when we forgive others!

DAY THREE: RAVENOUS PRAYER

MAIN IDEA

God wants us to keep asking, seeking, and knocking on heaven's door when we go to Him in prayer.

SUPPLIES NEEDED

- Small notebooks
- Markers
- Colored duct tape (especially camouflage)
- Child-safe scissors
- Stickers

CRAFT
PRAYER JOURNALS

Hand out one plain notebook to each child and encourage the children to decorate the cover to reflect their personality. Encourage them to use markers, strips of colored duct tape, or stickers in their work. As they are doing so, explain that a journal is a simple and easy way for them to keep track of their prayer requests. For instance, they might want to use their journals to later . . .

• Write out their personal prayer requests
• Write out their prayers for others
• Add photos/drawings of people they want to pray for
• Draw pictures of something they want to pray about each day
• Write out their favorite Bible verses
• Keep track (with a red pen) when God answers their prayers

Close your time by reminding the children that our prayers are important to God, so they should keep this journal somewhere in their home where they will see it and write in it every day.

DAY FOUR: REAL OBEDIENCE

MAIN IDEA

Obeying our parents pleases God and is a great way to honor Him.

SUPPLIES NEEDED

• White paper plates (9-inch)
• Paint

CRAFT
PAPER PLATE ART

Hand out the paper plates and have the children paint a picture for their parents of ways that they can obey Mom and Dad. When they are finished, they can also paint a portrait of their moms' and dads' happy, happy, happy faces when they obey. Close your time by stating that obeying our parents not only pleases them but also pleases God.

DAY FIVE: ROWDY KINDNESS

MAIN IDEA

There are many little ways that we can show kindness to others each day!

SUPPLIES NEEDED

• Large roll of mural-sized paper
• Paint
• Markers

CRAFT
KINDNESS MURAL

For your final activity at Korie's Craft Shed, roll out the large roll of white paper and ask the entire class to paint a mural of people being kind to each other. The children can work together as a team to create one large picture or can work individually and draw smaller scenes. When they are finished, put the mural up on the wall for all to enjoy. Close by explaining to the group that as this mural shows, there are many little ways that we can show rowdy kindness to those around us each and every day.

THE WAREHOUSE

Anyone who has watched *Duck Dynasty*® knows that the Duck Commander warehouse is the place where Jase, Martin, Godwin, and Jep try to make their work more fun. It's also the place where they bond as family.

To this end, at this station the kids will play fun team-building games that will help them grow closer as friends and help them gain a better understanding of God's plan for their lives.

THE WAREHOUSE ROTATION SCHEDULE

TIME	GROUP 1	GROUP 2	GROUP 3	GROUP 4	GROUP 5
9:00–9:25 am 5:30–5:55 pm	Opening Roundup	Opening Roundup	Opening Roundup	Opening Roundup	Opening Roundup
9:30–9:55 am 6:00–6:25 pm	Missy's Music and Memory	Si's Bull Pen	Miss Kay's Kitchen	The Warehouse	Korie's Craft Shed
10:00–10:25 am 6:30–6:55 pm	Korie's Craft Shed	Missy's Music and Memory	Si's Bull Pen	Miss Kay's Kitchen	The Warehouse
10:30–10:55 am 7:00–7:25 pm	The Warehouse	Korie's Craft Shed	Missy's Music and Memory	Si's Bull Pen	Miss Kay's Kitchen
11:00–11:25 am 7:30–7:55 pm	Miss Kay's Kitchen	The Warehouse	Korie's Craft Shed	Missy's Music and Memory	Si's Bull Pen
11:30–11:55 am 8:00–8:25 pm	Si's Bull Pen	Miss Kay's Kitchen	The Warehouse	Korie's Craft Shed	Missy's Music and Memory
12:00–12:15 pm 8:30–8:45 pm	Closing Roundup	Closing Roundup	Closing Roundup	Closing Roundup	Closing Roundup

SETTING UP THE STATION

For your Duck Commander warehouse, you need to have an open space with plenty of room for the children to move around (a gym or even an outdoor location will work well for many of the games). You can decorate the walls of the room with pictures of the guys and a sign that says "Duck Commander," just like the one at the warehouse in West Monroe. To make this station more fun, have your actors playing Jase, Martin, and Godwin wear their beards and help out. They could even wear nametags to help the children identify them. As "Willie," wear your trademark bandana, plaid shirt, and brown beard. Keep the children's safety in mind when setting up the equipment, and make sure none of the kids gets too rambunctious during their time at this station. Be sure to clearly explain the rules of the games before you begin and what your expectations are for their behavior and consideration of the other players.

MASTER EQUIPMENT LIST

The following is a complete list of the equipment that you will need to do each of the games described in this section. Note that there are several games listed for each day, so depending on the ages of your children and the number of games you want to play, you might not need every item on this list.

- 2 stick horses (you can purchase these or make your own from old mop or broom handles)
- Several barrels or chairs
- Masking tape
- 10 empty one-liter soft drink bottles
- 4–6 soft-foam dodge balls
- A whistle or duck call
- Rubber ducks or smaller balls (such as tennis balls)
- A large piece of fabric or a towel
- Blindfolds (bandanas work well)
- A bucket filled with different colored balls
- A camo vest or jacket
- Camo pants
- A few pairs of sunglasses
- Strips of cloth or bandages

DAY ONE: REDONKULOUS FAITH

MAIN IDEA

Teamwork requires putting your faith in another person, just as trusting God requires you to put your faith in Him.

GAME #1
BARREL RACES (ALL AGES)

For this game, you will need at least two stick horses, several barrels or chairs, and masking tape. Ahead of time, set up the barrels or chairs around the room, making sure that there is enough room for the children to safely maneuver around them. Tear off a strip of masking tape and place it on the floor to indicate the starting line.

Explain to the children that today they will be doing a relay race with the stick horses. Break the kids into two teams and have them line up behind the starting line. When you say "go," the first person is to "ride" his or her stick horse through the course, navigating the various obstacles that you have set up. They must keep the stick between their legs, just as if they were riding a real horse. The team that completes the course first is the winner. Play additional rounds as desired, adding more/different obstacles to make it more interesting for the children.

GAME #2
WILLIE'S BOWLING ALLEY (ALL AGES)

For this game, you will need ten empty one-liter soft drink bottles, masking tape, and a basketball (or similar heavy ball). Fill up each of the bottles with a little bit of water (make sure not to fill the bottles up too much, as you want them to be weighted down but not impossible for the kids to knock over). Set up your "pins" at one end of the room and tear off a strip of masking tape to serve as the fault line that the kids shouldn't cross. Have the children line up and give the first person the ball. Have the person roll the ball down the "lane" and see how many pins he or she can knock down. Declare the person who knocked down the most pins at the end to be the winner. (As an option, you can set up two sets of pins so more kids can play at the same time.)

GAME #3
WHO'S THE TALLEST (ALL AGES)

This is another excellent game that will teach the children how to work together. Instruct the students that you will give them three minutes to put themselves in order of shortest to tallest. The only catch is that they can't say a word to one another during this time. Do not help the children as they do this and call time when the three minutes is up. Discuss as a group what it took for them to make this happen (*someone had to take charge, everyone had to do his or her part, they had to help those who weren't sure what to do*). Close by discussing how putting their faith in one another played a part in their success or failure in this task and how we can choose to put our faith in God each day.

DAY TWO: RADICAL FORGIVENESS

MAIN IDEA

As the Parable of the Unmerciful Servant shows, we must always choose to forgive those who have wronged us.

GAME #1
DUCKS AND DECOYS (ALL AGES)

This game is a hyped-up version of the old game Simon Says and a version of a newer game called Ships and Sailors. Explain to the group that you are "the Boss" and that you will be calling out various commands that they need to follow. The first command you will be giving is, "Boss is coming." Whenever they hear this command, they must stand at attention and salute until you give the command, "at ease." If any of the players talk or break attention before you give the command, they will be out of the game. In addition, if they respond to any other command you give before you say "at ease," they will also be out of the game. Go over each of the commands you will give as the Boss so the group knows the required response:

- Boss is coming: the children stand still at attention and salute.
- Ducks flying north: the children flap their arms and run in a designated direction.
- Ducks flying south: the children flap their arms and run in the opposite direction.
- Duck decoys: the children crouch down and put their arms up like the head of a duck.

- Cut 'em all, Jack: the children act as if they're shooting at ducks flying in the air.
- Merciful king: the children get in pairs. One person says, "I can't pay!" while the other pats the person on the back and says, "That's okay."
- Unmerciful servant: the children get in pairs. One person says, "I can't pay" while the other shakes his or her finger and says, "Off to jail!"
- Four boys eating: the children must get four people in a group, sit down, and pretend to eat.
- Beards are back: the children put both their hands under their chin and wiggle their fingers.
- Uncle Si is nappin': the children lie on the ground for a pretend nap.
- Three men paddling a *perot*: the children must get three people in a group, sit down, and pretend they are rowing a boat.
- Happy, happy, happy: the children clap their hands and smile.
- Sadie says hi: the children put their hands on their hips, wave, and say, "Hi, y'all!"
- Forgive your neighbor: the children pat each other on the shoulders.

Play the game by giving these commands in any order. Eliminate any players who do not respond quickly enough (before you give the next command), who move before the "at ease" command, who do not have the required number of participants in their groups, or who do not completely follow the command. When a player is eliminated, have all the children say, "He gone!" The winner is the last player still standing at the end. As an option, you can have any of the children play the role of the Boss, or you can make up more of your own commands.

GAME #2
DUCK HUNT DODGE BALL (OLDER CHILDREN)

For this high-energy game, you will need a whistle (or duck call), four to six soft-foam dodge balls, and a good-sized room or outdoor location. Begin by breaking the group into two separate teams and specifying the boundaries in which the game will be played. Place the dodge balls together in the center of the floor and select two to four "hunters" to stand in the center with the balls. The rest of the students will be the "ducks" and need to form a big circle around the hunters.

When the duck call is blown, the ducks should fly around while the hunters try to hit them with the dodge balls. When a duck is hit, the player must say, "Quack, I forgive you!" and sit down on the ground. Only the hunters are allowed to throw the dodge balls. After a few minutes, blow the duck call/whistle and select other children to be the hunters. Be sure to remind the kids of the ground rules, and pull out any child who is acting too aggressively toward the other kids. Have fun!

GAME #3
DUCKS FLYING OVER AND UNDER (YOUNGER CHILDREN)

This is a simple relay game that your younger children will especially enjoy. You will need some small rubber ducks or, if none are available, some small balls to serve as ducks (tennis balls or playground balls work well). Make sure you have enough ducks/balls for the number of teams you intend to have. Begin by dividing the group into teams of about six or eight people. Have the teams line up in a straight line and all face the same direction.

When you say "go," the first player will hand the ball/duck *over* his or her head to the second player, who must pass it *under* his or her legs to the third player, who again passes it *over* his or her head. The winner is the team who gets the duck/ball to the back of the line first. When you are finished, explain that forgiving one another is much like this game—we "pass the duck" to the next person and choose not to hold anything against that person. Play as many rounds as time allows.

DAY THREE: RAVENOUS PRAYER

MAIN IDEA

God is available to talk with at any time, and He wants to hear from us. We just have to figure out how to not let distractions get in our way.

GAME #1
STEAL THE DECOY (ALL AGES)

For this game, you will need to place a large piece of fabric or a towel in the center of the room to represent the "decoy." Explain that when the Robertsons are out duck hunting, they use a decoy to distract the ducks so they can move in closer. Today, the group will be attempting to "steal" this decoy.

Divide the group members into two teams. Have each team line up on opposite sides of the room, facing the other team. Have each person count off on his or her team so that each team has a player who represents #1, #2, #3, and so forth. You or another rodeo hand will then call out a number, and the players who have that number on each team will race to the center to steal the decoy. The player must grab the towel and then run back to his or her team before the other player tags him or her. Award points when a player gets back to his or her line without being tagged.

To add some excitement to the game, you can call more than one number at a time. Conclude by stating that when we pray, Satan will try to distract us with all kinds of things, much like the decoy. We have to learn how to "steal away" those distractions so we can "steal away" and spend time with God.

GAME #2
ANIMAL CONNECTION (ALL AGES)

Explain to the children that you are going to call out four different kinds of animals, and you want them to move into the group of the animal with which they most closely identify. The animals are: deer, duck, squirrel, and frog. Once they are in their groups, discuss the following questions:

1. Why do you identify the most with this group?
2. What is one thing this animal is afraid of?
3. What is one thing you're afraid of?
4. How can you take your fears to God in prayer?

GAME #3
SIT DOWN IF . . . (ALL AGES)

Start this game by asking all the children to stand. Read the following list and ask the children to sit down when the statement applies to them.

1. Sit down if you ate eggs this morning.
2. Sit down if you are wearing blue.
3. Sit down if you were born in March.
4. Sit down if you are the oldest child in your family.
5. Sit down if you saw the movie *Home Alone*.
6. Sit down if you have blue eyes.
7. Sit down if you take piano lessons.
8. Sit down if you've been to Disney World.
9. Sit down if you have broken a bone.
10. Sit down if you didn't pray to God today.

Declare the last person standing to be the winner. Add your own "sit down" instructions if needed and create additional lists to play the game more than once. Close by stating that God knows everything about us—including whether we ate eggs for breakfast this morning or if we have blue eyes. We can talk to God at any time throughout the day and share what is happening in our lives, just as we would do with our friends at school.

DAY FOUR: REAL OBEDIENCE

MAIN IDEA

God doesn't ask us to obey Him because He likes to see us move around obstacles. Instead, He gives us instructions for our own good.

GAME #1
JUST LIKE THE ROBERTSONS (ALL AGES)

Have the group members sit in chairs in a circle. Tell the children that you are going to call out some things that the Robertsons have done or like to do, and if they also like or have done these things, they need to move one chair to the right. Here is the list:

- Have been to Disney World.
- Have been to Hawaii.
- Saw the movie *Elf*.
- Caught a fish.
- Rode a four-wheeler.
- Baked a cake with no help.
- Rode a horse.
- Ate alligator.
- Slept outside.
- Have gone hunting.
- Played basketball in school.
- Have gone snow skiing.
- Have been to the beach.
- Have an uncle like Si.
- Caught a frog.
- Like ice cream.
- Played football in school.
- Lost their cell phone.
- Have practiced shooting a gun.
- Have been to summer camp.
- Have told someone else about Jesus.
- Have obeyed their parents even when it was hard to do.
- Have more than two brothers or sisters.
- Said a prayer before they ate breakfast this morning.
- Can do a cartwheel.

Add your own ideas to this list. As the game progresses, the players will likely end up sitting on someone else's lap. The one to get around the circle first is the winner. Conclude by stating that while we might not have done all the things the Robertsons have done on this list, three things we can all do is pray, obey our parents, and share with others about Jesus. God loves it when we obey and follow Him!

GAME #2
BLIND OBEDIENCE OBSTACLE COURSE (OLDER CHILDREN)

For this game, you will need to set up an obstacle coursing using chairs, tables, benches, cones, buckets, balls, and other items. You will also need at least one blindfold. (Make sure to set up the obstacle course in a way that is safe for a child with a blindfold to be able to move through without getting injured.)

Explain that you are going to choose one person to be the "caller," and that person will need to call out instructions to the blindfolded person on how to navigate the course. Place the caller halfway down the course and blindfold the first participant. The caller will need to call out directions for the blindfolded person to take to move through the course. After completing the course, the player becomes the caller, and the caller goes to the end of the line. Play until all children have had a turn. For more intense options:

1. *Have two teams working through the course at the same time.* The blindfolded player must determine whom they should listen to and obey. (There are a lot of good spiritual lessons that you can apply from this option!)
2. *Add a bucket to the obstacle course that is filled with different colored balls.* The caller must

get the participant to select the right color ball before he or she can move forward.

3. *Allow hecklers from the crowd to distract the players.* This will become difficult and frustrating for the players, but is a great lesson on having to work to obey the correct voice.

GAME #3
MISS KAY'S IN THE KITCHEN (YOUNGER CHILDREN)

Begin this game by having the children sit in a circle. The first child will say, "Miss Kay's in the kitchen, and she has _____." The child will need to fill in the blank with an item from a kitchen, such as "butter," "flour," or "a spoon." The next child in line will then repeat the phrase and add an additional item to the list. This will continue until everyone has had a turn. For example:

First player: "Miss Kay's in the kitchen, and she has a *spoon*."
Second player: "Miss Kay's in the kitchen, and she has a *spoon* and a *bowl*."
Third player: "Miss Kay's in the kitchen, and she has a *spoon*, a *bowl*, and some *flour*."

Eliminate any players who cannot remember the items in order and declare the last person standing to be the winner. Congratulate the children for obeying your instructions and doing their best to remember the items in order. State that unlike this game, God doesn't ask us to follow long, ridiculous lists of instructions. His commands are always for our own good, and He wants us to obey Him so we will lead happy, happy, happy lives!

DAY FIVE: ROWDY KINDNESS

MAIN IDEA

There are always people in our lives to whom we can show kindness. When we do, it not only helps the other person, but it can help us as well!

GAME #1
BLIND HUNTING DOG (ALL AGES)

To play this game, you will need 3 tennis balls per number of teams you have. For example, if you have 40 children with 8 players on a team, you will have 5 teams and will need 15 balls. You will also need one small container (a tennis ball container works well) per team and a blindfold. Begin by putting the children into teams of 6–8 players. Tell them that they are going on a duck hunt, and they need to choose one teammate who will be the Blind Hunting Dog.

Put the blindfold on the Blind Hunting Dog and explain that the ducks have fallen into the water and need to be retrieved. The Blind Hunting Dog will need to listen closely to his or her teammates to find the ducks. When all the players are blindfolded, release the balls on the other side of the room (enough for each team to get three). The Blind Hunting Dog will need to retrieve three balls by listening to the instructions of his or her teammates. When the Blind Hunting Dog retrieves all the balls, he or she will go back to his or her team, and the next person will take a turn being

blindfolded. The team who gets through all their players first is the winner.

When the game is over, ask the winning team how being kind to one another and calling out the correct instructions helped them to win. Discuss with the group different ways that they can show kindness to others. Ask a few volunteers to explain how being kind to others will not only help the other person but will also help them.

GAME #2
CAMO RELAY RACE (OLDER CHILDREN)

For this game, you will need masking tape, several pieces of hunting clothing (such as a camo vest or jacket, camo pants, a few pairs of sunglasses, and a bandana), and six strips of cloth or bandages. Make sure you have one item of each piece of hunting clothing and three bandages per team. Divide the children into two teams and have them designate one person to be the Injured Man in the parable told today. The rest of the group will be the Good Samaritans.

Place the articles of clothing in two separate piles at one end of the room and tear off a strip of masking tape to serve as the starting line. Have the Good Samaritans line up while the Injured Man stands off to the side a bit. When you say "go," the first person will run down to the pile, grab an item of clothing, run back to the starting line, and put it on the Injured Man. The Injured Man must wear the item correctly before the next person in line can proceed. The next Good Samaritan then runs down to the pile, heads back, and helps the Injured Man put on the article. This continues until all the Good Samaritans have had a turn and the team is sitting down. Make sure that they do not injure the Injured Man as they race to do this!

Conclude by stating that in the story today, the Good Samaritan showed kindness to the Injured Man by putting bandages on his wounds and taking care of him. In the same way, Jesus wants us to show kindness to those around us.

GAME #3
DUCK, DUCK, HUNTER (YOUNGER CHILDREN)

This game is played just like Duck, Duck, Goose. One child will be the Duck while the other children will be the Hunters sitting in a circle. The Duck will circle the group while tapping each child on the head, saying either "Duck" or "Hunter." When the Duck says the word "Hunter" and taps a child's head, that child will chase the Duck around the circle and try to tag him or her before the Duck gets back to his or her place in the circle. The game continues with the new Duck.

If you have a lot of kids in your group, you can have a circle inside a circle and have two games going at a time. You could even add a third circle if you're brave enough! This twist can bring new life to an old favorite game. Conclude by stating that we don't have to go on a hunt to find people to whom we can show kindness. God places people in our lives who need help each day—and we just need to look for them!

MISS KAY'S KITCHEN

Everyone in the Robertsons' neighborhood loves to go to Miss Kay's kitchen—and she loves to have company! In the same way, your Miss Kay's Kitchen will serve as a place the kids will love to go to get some snacks and spend some time working on their Bible memory verse. Miss Kay loves the Bible, and your children will walk away with a snack in their tummies and a Scripture verse in their hearts! As with the other rotations, you do not need to be an expert cook to lead this station (the recipes are simple), nor do you need any special gifting in acting (the scripts and object lessons are short).

MISS KAY'S KITCHEN ROTATION SCHEDULE

TIME	GROUP 1	GROUP 2	GROUP 3	GROUP 4	GROUP 5
9:00–9:25 am 5:30–5:55 pm	Opening Roundup	Opening Roundup	Opening Roundup	Opening Roundup	Opening Roundup
9:30–9:55 am 6:00–6:25 pm	Missy's Music and Memory	Si's Bull Pen	Miss Kay's Kitchen	The Warehouse	Korie's Craft Shed
10:00–10:25 am 6:30–6:55 pm	Korie's Craft Shed	Missy's Music and Memory	Si's Bull Pen	Miss Kay's Kitchen	The Warehouse
10:30–10:55 am 7:00–7:25 pm	The Warehouse	Korie's Craft Shed	Missy's Music and Memory	Si's Bull Pen	Miss Kay's Kitchen
11:00–11:25 am 7:30–7:55 pm	Miss Kay's Kitchen	The Warehouse	Korie's Craft Shed	Missy's Music and Memory	Si's Bull Pen
11:30–11:55 am 8:00–8:25 pm	Si's Bull Pen	Miss Kay's Kitchen	The Warehouse	Korie's Craft Shed	Missy's Music and Memory
12:00–12:15 am 8:30–8:45 pm	Closing Roundup	Closing Roundup	Closing Roundup	Closing Roundup	Closing Roundup

SETTING UP THE STATION

As "Miss Kay," you need to be dressed in an apron and wear a black wig (dimples optional). The ideal location for this station would be a café or kitchen area in your building—having a sink nearby for cleanup is handy—but any classroom will do. You will need to do very little setup to turn this area into Miss Kay's Kitchen, but as with the other stations you could put up pictures of Miss Kay (full-color or gray-scale; see DVD-ROM) or any other duck- or family-related items (duck pictures, duck call whistles, pictures of the Robertson boys). Also bring in kitchen-type items (utensils, pans, jars of spices) to give the station a more authentic feel.

As with Korie's Craft Shed, if you are concerned about spills, cover the tabletops with plastic tablecloths and tape them underneath to keep them from sliding off. You might also want to cover carpets and any other area that you want to keep food-free with large plastic tarps. Be sure to check before each session if any of the children in your group have food allergies (such as peanut or gluten allergies) or other special needs (such as diabetes). Finally, make sure that the kids wash their hands before the snack time begins and again when it ends, or provide hand sanitizer for them to use.

MASTER SUPPLIES LIST

Here is a complete list of the supplies that you will need to do each of the cooking projects described in the next section:

- Small white or brown sacks
- Premade heart-shaped sugar cookies
- Cans of red icing
- Ritz crackers
- Cheese spread
- Peanut butter
- Raisins
- Peanuts
- Dried cereal (such as Cheerios)
- M&M's
- Pretzels
- Popcorn
- Small bowls or cups
- Plastic resealable bags
- Chocolate pudding (1 four-ounce box)

- Frozen Cool Whip (1 small tub, thawed)
- Oreo cookies
- Gummy worms
- Teddy Grahams (cinnamon, chocolate, and graham cracker flavored)
- Plastic knives, forks, and spoons
- Drink of choice
- Paper cups and napkins
- Hand sanitizer

DAY ONE: REDONKULOUS FAITH

MAIN IDEA

Following God requires a "redonkulous" amount of faith!

BIBLE STORY

The Parable of the Sower (Matthew 13:1–23).

MEMORY VERSE
1 CORINTHIANS 16:13

Preschool and Early Elementary: "Be on your guard. Stand firm in the faith."

Later Elementary: "Be on your guard. Stand firm in the faith. Be brave. Be strong."

SUPPLIES NEEDED

- Small white or brown sacks
- Premade heart-shaped sugar cookies
- Cans of red icing

- Plastic knives
- Drink of choice
- Paper cups and napkins

PREPARATION

Ahead of time, place the sugar cookies into the sacks.

SCRIPT FOR MISS KAY

Our lesson today is called "redonkulous faith." Now, what do you think "redonkulous" means? *(Let some of the children respond.)* It's a crazy made-up word that means a big or over-the-top kind of faith — like bigger-than-an-elephant kind of faith! Now, what does "faith" mean? *(Let some of the children respond.)* Faith is trusting in things we can't always see. Let me explain what I mean.

When I cook something new, I follow the recipe just the way it is written. When I do, I have faith that it will turn out just like it is supposed to. Of course, I don't know for sure that it will, but I have *faith* that it will. What are some things that *you* put *your* faith in? How about that when you turn on the faucet, water will come out? Or that when you turn on your stove, it will light? Or that when you sit down in a chair, it will support you?

We trust some things to work because God created them to function as they do — like fire and water. We trust other things to work because we have experienced them working in the past — like those chairs. Faith comes from experiencing something and trusting it will be that way again. Now, let's put this to the test today. Your snack is hidden in a paper sack, and you have to have faith in *me* that I have given you something good. So … do you trust me?

(Pass out the sacks and ask the children to wait to open them until everyone has received a sack. Now have them look into their sack.) Well, I hope you had faith in me, because our snack today is a heart-shaped cookie. This cookie will help you remember that having faith comes from the heart. When we love God, we trust Him to do what is best for us, and our love for God leads to faith in Him. So, this week, I want you to look for the things God is showing you to make your faith stronger. Maybe it's a beautiful flower or a rainbow, a new baby or a hug from your grandparents. Maybe someone you know was healed from a sickness. Just open your eyes and be ready, and God will show you His goodness.

Now, each day this week during our snack time I am going to ask you to work on your Scripture memory verse. Today as we do so, I am going to hand out some red icing and plastic knives so you can decorate your heart cookie. *(Hand out the plastic knives and allow the children to place the icing on their cookies. Ask each person in the group if he or she can recite the memory verse for the day.)*

DAY TWO: RADICAL FORGIVENESS

MAIN IDEA

God wants us to forgive others in a radical way!

BIBLE STORY

The Parable of the Unmerciful Servant (Matthew 18:21–35).

MEMORY VERSE
COLOSSIANS 3:13

Preschool and Early Elementary: "Forgive, just as the Lord forgave you."

Later Elementary: "Put up with each other. Forgive the things you are holding against one another. Forgive, just as the Lord forgave you."

SUPPLIES NEEDED

- Ritz crackers
- Cheese spread
- Peanut butter
- Plastic knives
- Napkins or small plates
- Drink of choice
- Paper cups

PREPARATION

Today's snack involves peanut butter, so be sure to check for food allergies before each session begins. If any child is allergic to peanut butter, he or she can use the cheese spread instead.

Raising four boys was sometimes hard. Can you think of reasons why it might be hard? *(Let the children respond.)* Yes, sometimes they would fight and argue. One time, Jase and Willie got in a fight over making toast and pizza. Can you believe that? I wasn't home that day, so I was glad they had a friend there to help them out and tell them they were acting silly. The boys had to apologize to each other and forgive each other.

It takes a lot of forgiveness to live in a big family and not hold a grudge against your family members, but God will help you. One way I have found that helps me forgive a person is to pray for him or her. After all, it's hard to stay mad at someone you are praying for! Our memory verse for the day says we should forgive as the Lord forgives us. Yes, that's right—the Lord forgives each of us every day when we don't live the way He wants us to live. Because God forgives us, we should forgive others. So let's work this week to forgive our friends, our brothers, our sisters, and even our parents.

Now, who here can tell me what our story is for the day? *(Let the children respond.)* It's called the Parable of the Unmerciful Servant. As you might remember, in that story a king forgave a huge debt that one of his servants owed him. But then that same man went and demanded another servant to pay back a small amount that he owed him. When the king found out, he was angry that the man he had forgiven had not in turn forgiven the servant who owed him money.

In those days, the people used silver coins to pay back their debts. Today our snack is going to be Ritz crackers, which look a bit like those coins. I am going to hand out some peanut butter and/or cheese spread for you to put on your crackers. As you eat these, I want you to think about how God loves you and forgives you. *(Hand out the Ritz crackers, plastic knives, peanut butter, and/ or cheese spread, and allow the children to smear their crackers. Ask each person in the group if he or she can recite the memory verse for the day.)*

DAY THREE: RAVENOUS PRAYER

MAIN IDEA

God listens to our prayers and delights in providing for our needs.

BIBLE STORY

The Parable of the Friend in Need (Luke 11:5–10).

MEMORY VERSE
PHILIPPIANS 4:6

Preschool and Early Elementary: "Tell God about everything. Ask and pray. Give thanks to him."

Later Elementary: "Don't worry about anything. Instead, tell God about everything. Ask and pray. Give thanks to him."

SUPPLIES NEEDED

- Raisins
- Peanuts
- Dried cereal (such as Cheerios)
- M&M's
- Pretzels
- Popcorn
- Small bowls
- Plastic resealable bags
- Drink of choice
- Paper cups

PREPARATION

Put the ingredients in separate bowls so the children can make their own "power snacks." Place a small spoon in each bowl so the students will keep the portions fairly small.

SCRIPT FOR MISS KAY

Today's Bible story was about a man who knocked on the door of a neighbor and asked to get some food for his hungry friend. As you recall, that man kept on knocking until his friend finally opened the door! This story is a parable about how we are to pray to God. God loves to take care of us, and when we ask Him to meet our needs, He will do it! Our prayers to God are like knocking on His great, big door. God will always open His door and listen to us. However, sometimes He wants us to keep on knocking and asking. That's what we call "persistence."

Do you know what a "power source" is? *(Let the children respond.)* Well, a power source is anything that gives something power. An example is a cellphone charger. When you plug your cellphone into the charger, your cellphone will get more energy. God is your power source, and when you "plug into" that source by praying and reading the Bible, He gives you the power to do everything you need to do. If you need God to give you strength, ask Him. If you need God to give you peace, ask Him. If you need God to give you wisdom, ask Him.

Our memory verse for the day says to not be anxious about anything, because God will take care of whatever we are facing if we ask Him. That means we really don't have to worry about anything, because our God is such a big God that He can handle anything we need Him to handle. But He does want us to ask Him. He wants us to know that we need Him. Remember, He is our power source.

Today's snack is a "power snack" because it is full of good things that give us energy to get through the day, just as God does. I am going to hand out each of the ingredients, and I want you to put together your own "trail mix" to serve as your power snack. As you eat this, I want you to remember that God always gives us power when we go to Him in prayer and read the Bible. *(Hand out the bowls you premade with all of the ingredients and the plastic bags. Have the children select the items they want from the bowls and put them into their bags for their power snack. Ask each person in the group if he or she can recite the memory verse for the day.)*

DAY FOUR: REAL OBEDIENCE

MAIN IDEA

Sometimes it might seem like no fun when God asks us to obey, but we have to remember that it is for our own benefit and our own good.

BIBLE STORY

The Parable of the Two Sons (Matthew 21:28–32).

MEMORY VERSE
2 JOHN 1:6

Preschool and Early Elementary: "The way we show our love is to obey God's commands."

Later Elementary: "The way we show our love is to obey God's commands. He commands you to lead a life of love."

SUPPLIES NEEDED

- Chocolate pudding (1 four-ounce box)
- Frozen Cool Whip (1 small tub, thawed)
- Oreo cookies
- Gummy worms
- Bowls or cups
- Plastic spoons

PREPARATION

You will need to make this dessert ahead of time. Prepare the chocolate pudding following the directions on the package. Crush the Oreo cookies and put ½ cup into the pudding. Stir in the tub of Cool Whip. Spoon the mixture into small cups and top with a couple of gummy worms and more crushed cookies. Refrigerate until served. This recipe makes approximately 10 cups, but if you use smaller cups, it could make 20. Adjust to your group size.

SCRIPT FOR MISS KAY

Today's lesson is about obedience. Think of all the people you are asked to obey. Can you name some of them? *(Let the children respond.)* That's right—your parents, your teachers, your principal, your grandparents, and your aunts and uncles. Do you think God considers obedience to be important? *(Let the children respond.)* I think He does. Learning to obey is especially important because it can save us from lots of trouble. Let me explain.

Imagine that you were about to step on a snake and your mom yelled, "Stop!" Now, if you were not used to obeying her, you might ignore what she had to say and stepped right down on that snake. But if you were used to being obedient, you would follow her command right away and avoid a lot of pain. In the same way, God commands us to obey Him because He knows what is best for us. He makes it clear in the Bible that His rules for good living are not meant to keep us from having fun. He made those rules because they are good for us, and if we follow them we will have a happier life.

Our parable today is about two sons who were asked to work in the garden. One didn't want to work, but he did so anyway. The other said he would gladly go, but he didn't. The son who did work—even if he had a bad attitude about it—was more pleasing to his father because he obeyed. Now, I know that your parents ask you to do things all the time and sometimes you don't want to do what they ask. But God says you are to obey your parents and that when you do, it makes Him happy.

Our snack today is called a "dirt dessert." While that might sound gross, I think you will like it. As you eat this snack, I want you to think about the two brothers in the parable who were asked to work in the garden. I want you to remember that God wants you to always be obedient to your parents. *(Hand out the premade desserts. As the children are eating, ask each person in the group if he or she can recite the memory verse for the day.)*

DAY FIVE: ROWDY KINDNESS

— MAIN IDEA —

God wants us to be loud and rowdy when it comes to being kind to others!

— BIBLE STORY —

The Parable of the Good Samaritan (Luke 10:25–37).

MEMORY VERSE
COLOSSIANS 3:12

Preschool and Early Elementary: "Put on tender mercy and kindness as if they were your clothes."

Later Elementary: "You are God's chosen people. You are holy and dearly loved. So put on tender mercy and kindness as if they were your clothes. Don't be proud. Be gentle and patient."

— SUPPLIES NEEDED —

- Teddy Grahams (cinnamon, chocolate, and graham cracker flavored)
- Plates or small bowls
- Drink of choice
- Paper cups

(Begin by showing the three different types of Teddy Grahams.) Look at these fun Teddy Grahams. There are three different flavors here: cinnamon, chocolate, and graham cracker. Let's see which one is your favorite. Raise your hand if you like the chocolate kind. *(Let the children respond.)* Now raise your hand if you like the cinnamon kind. *(Let the children respond.)* Okay, who likes the graham cracker kind? *(Let the children respond.)*

It's fun to see how we all like different things. God made each of us special and different. What are some ways God made people different? *(Let the children respond.)* Great answers—yes, we all have different hair color, different heights, and different eye colors. We're different sizes, and our voices are different. We're all different just like these Teddy Grahams. And just because someone is different, it doesn't mean we don't like that person or should treat him or her in an unkind way. Our job is to love *everyone* no matter what. That's what God does. He loves all of us just the same.

Being kind to others is a decision we have to make each day because every day someone might make us angry or mad. God doesn't want us to act ugly just because we're mad. In fact, He challenges us to act with kindness no matter what happens to us. That might be hard, but you can do it!

Our memory verse today says to put on kindness as if it were our clothes. That's a funny way to think about it, isn't it? God is telling us to "put on" kindness like we put on a sweater or a shirt. To wear it! I like that idea. Do you? If we all put on our "kindness" clothes before we left the house each morning, just think how much better the world would be. Do you know what? You and I can help change the world by choosing to be kind. What we do does make a difference. So let's do it! *(Hand out the Teddy Grahams and let the kids choose the flavors they like. As the children are eating, ask each person in the group if he or she can recite the memory verse for the day. Note that this is a fun food activity that you can take deeper, depending on the ages of your students. For the older kids, you could discuss how to be kind on the phone or why bullying is such as problem.)*

SI'S BULL PEN

This station is so named because Si loves to "shoot the bull" with everyone around him. During this rotation, the students will have time to work on activity sheets that have been especially designed to reinforce the main lesson of the day. They will enjoy listening to Si give some little-known but interesting Bible facts (for both older and younger children) and dive into God's Word themselves to find some of the answers.

SI'S BULL PEN ROTATION SCHEDULE

TIME	GROUP 1	GROUP 2	GROUP 3	GROUP 4	GROUP 5
9:00 – 9:25 am 5:30 – 5:55 pm	Opening Roundup	Opening Roundup	Opening Roundup	Opening Roundup	Opening Roundup
9:30 – 9:55 am 6:00 – 6:25 pm	Missy's Music and Memory	Si's Bull Pen	Miss Kay's Kitchen	The Warehouse	Korie's Craft Shed
10:00 – 10:25 am 6:30 – 6:55 pm	Korie's Craft Shed	Missy's Music and Memory	Si's Bull Pen	Miss Kay's Kitchen	The Warehouse
10:30 – 10:55 am 7:00 – 7:25 pm	The Warehouse	Korie's Craft Shed	Missy's Music and Memory	Si's Bull Pen	Miss Kay's Kitchen
11:00 – 11:25 am 7:30 – 7:55 pm	Miss Kay's Kitchen	The Warehouse	Korie's Craft Shed	Missy's Music and Memory	Si's Bull Pen
11:30 – 11:55 am 8:00 – 8:25 pm	Si's Bull Pen	Miss Kay's Kitchen	The Warehouse	Korie's Craft Shed	Missy's Music and Memory
12:00 – 12:15 am 8:30 – 8:45 pm	Closing Roundup	Closing Roundup	Closing Roundup	Closing Roundup	Closing Roundup

SETTING UP THE STATION

As "Si," you need to be dressed in a camo cap, T-shirt (ideally a Duck Commander T-shirt), camo shirt, glasses, gray beard, and you should carry a plastic cup. You will need a fairly quiet room with chairs and a table where the children can work on their activities. Decorate the room by putting up pictures of Si and the Robertsons on the wall, or mimic what you have done with the Duck Call Shop for the Opening and Closing Roundups. Another option is to make this room look like a real "bull pen," with barnyard equipment scattered around and even fake "fences" to keep in the bulls. If you go this route, you could even hang real rodeo gear (such as saddles and ropes) from the walls, or just find pictures of this type of gear.

Note that you will need to provide the group members with pencils, crayons, Bibles, and the provided reproducible activity sheets. Explain the instructions and help children, as needed.

Several "Si Facts" for each lesson have been provided, so choose the ones that are appropriate for the age of the students attending your rotation. As an option, feel free to adapt or change any of the facts to best meet the needs of your group. Read these facts as the children do their activity sheets or use the facts as discussion starters to take the group members deeper into the Bible.

DAY ONE: REDONKULOUS FAITH

MAIN IDEA

Following God requires a "redonkulous" amount of faith!

BIBLE STORY

The Parable of the Sower (Matthew 13:1–23).

SI'S LITTLE-KNOWN FACTS
FOR OLDER CHILDREN

- In Matthew 13:3 we read, "A farmer went to plant his seed." Back in Jesus's time, a farmer's garden might be miles from his home.
- Jesus talks about "thorns" in this parable. Sixteen varieties of thorny plants have been recorded as being in this area at the time Jesus told this story. Some are described as being so tall that a horse could not push through them.
- Wherever we see the words "faith" or "believe" in the New Testament, they are usually a translation from the original Greek root word *pistis*. The noun form of the word, *pistis*, is usually translated as "faith," while the verb form, *pisteuo*, is translated as "believe."
- Right after this parable, in Matthew 13:31–32, Jesus compares faith to a mustard seed. Mustard seeds are the small round seeds of various kinds of mustard plants, and they are usually only about one to two millimeters in diameter. That's about 1/20th of an inch in size.
- Hebrews 11 is generally known as the "faith chapter" because in it the author describes all kinds of great deeds of faith that people in the Bible performed.

SI'S LITTLE-KNOWN FACTS
FOR YOUNGER CHILDREN

- In Bible times, a farmer's garden might be a long way from his house. He would have to walk for many miles to get there!
- The story that Jesus told says there were "thorny" plants. A thorny plant would be like a rose that has thorns on it that can stick your finger—except they are probably not as pretty.
- During the time Jesus told this story, there were at least sixteen different kinds of thorny plants. Some were so big you wouldn't be able to ride a horse through them!
- The Bible is divided into many different "books." One good book on faith is Hebrews, which is part of the New Testament.

UNDERSTANDING FAITH

1. Read Hebrews 11:6 and write it in the space below.

2. What is something that seems "impossible" for you to do?

3. Think of one thing in which you have faith. Draw it in the space below.

4. Put a checkmark by the best definition of "faith":

   ❑ The name of a boy band
   ❑ Trusting in something or someone we are sure about
   ❑ Trusting in something or someone we are not sure about
   ❑ A flavor of ice cream

5. How often do you think about God?

   ❑ Every day
   ❑ Every hour
   ❑ Almost never

6. Look up James 1:6 – 7 in the Bible. Complete the verse:

But when you _____, you must _____ and not _____, because the

one who _____ is like a wave of the _____, blown and tossed by the _____.

That person should not expect to receive _____ from the Lord. (NIV)

FAITH IN GOD'S CREATION

INSTRUCTIONS: Look at the pictures. Circle and color the things that God created.

© Virinaflora/Shutterstock

DAY TWO: RADICAL FORGIVENESS

— MAIN IDEA —

God wants us to forgive others in a radical way!

— BIBLE STORY —

The Parable of the Unmerciful Servant (Matthew 18:21–35)

SI'S LITTLE-KNOWN FACTS
FOR OLDER CHILDREN

- In Jesus's time, Jewish law wouldn't have allowed a person to sell his wife and children to pay a debt.
- Even if a man could sell his wife and children, they would not have sold for the money the unmerciful servant needed to repay his debt to the king.
- Ten thousand talents would be about four billion dollars ($4,000,000,000) in today's money. Jesus used this figure of 10,000 talents to make the point that there was no way the servant could have repaid the debt.
- Jesus often told stories about the conditions of His time, and His listeners would have been very familiar with the facts. They would have understood 10,000 talents to be an enormous debt.
- The fellow servant's debt of 100 denarii was equivalent to $4,000 today. While that is still a lot of money, it is much less than $4,000,000,000!
- It was a common practice during the first

century to have a person thrown into prison until he could pay a debt.

SI'S LITTLE-KNOWN FACTS
FOR YOUNGER CHILDREN

- The Bible story we read today used the words "ten thousand talents." A talent was the money of that day, like we say dollars. Ten thousand talents would be about four billion today!
- The word "parable" is another word for story. Jesus told stories so the people would understand Him better.
- In Bible times, if someone couldn't pay a debt, he would often be sent to jail or prison.

ACTIVITY SHEET INSTRUCTIONS
FOR OLDER CHILDREN

Once you distribute the activity sheets to the children, tell them that they should think of some things that are needed for forgiveness to take place, at least one for each letter in the word "FORGIVE." Tell your group that each phase they brainstorm should start with a verb, because verbs are "action words" and forgiving others requires an action on our part. (You can write some samples on a whiteboard or poster board to get them started.)

Sample:

F — Forget the little things
O — Open your heart to others
R — Remember you need forgiveness too
G — Give others a second chance
I — Include God as your helper
V — Volunteer to apologize first
E — Encourage others to forgive

FORGIVENESS ACRONYM

F

O

R

G

I

V

E

FORGIVENESS

INSTRUCTIONS: Color happy faces on the children.

Forgiveness makes me ...

happy, happy, happy!

DAY THREE: RAVENOUS PRAYER

MAIN IDEA

God tells us in the Bible that we are to be persistent—or "ravenous"—in prayer!

BIBLE STORY

The Parable of the Friend in Need (Luke 11:5–10).

SI'S LITTLE-KNOWN FACTS
FOR OLDER CHILDREN

- In Jesus's day, bread was typically baked in the morning. If you ran out, the usual practice was to borrow some from a neighbor.
- However, you wouldn't borrow from a friend at night unless it was an emergency. People braced up their doors to keep thieves from breaking in, so it would be a huge hassle to open the door.
- Jesus told a similar parable in Luke 18:1–8 called the Parable of the Persistent Widow. In that parable, a widow came to a judge many times and kept pestering him until he granted her request.
- The most well-known prayer in the Bible is the Lord's Prayer, which is found in Matthew 6 and Luke 11.
- The Lord's Prayer, like much of the writing of its day, uses a two-four beat rhythm and rhyming. Because there were no tape recorders back then, this would have been a good way for people to remember what they heard.
- The word "amen" is from a Hebrew adverb meaning "so be it."
- The longest book in the Bible is Psalms. It contains 150 "psalms" or songs that are sometimes regarded as prayers.

SI'S LITTLE-KNOWN FACTS
FOR YOUNGER CHILDREN

- In Bible times, people often borrowed bread from their neighbors if they ran out. It was just something everyone did.
- People usually put boards over their doors at night to keep out robbers. So it would be hard to open the door for a friend at night.
- In Bible times, they didn't have ways to record what they said like we do today. So they had to memorize everything. Most things were written with a rhyme, like a poem, so it would be easier to learn.
- The Bible is divided into different books. The longest book is Psalms. It has 150 songs, or prayers.
- We end our prayers by saying "amen," which means, "so be it."

PRAYER THAT PLEASES GOD

1. Look up James 5:15–16 in the Bible and fill in the blanks:

And the _____ offered in _____ will make the sick person well; the

_____ will raise them up. If they have sinned, they will be _____.

Therefore _____ your sins to each other and _____ for each other so

that you may be healed. The _____ of a righteous person is _____

and _____. (NIV)

A good guideline for how to pray is known as the "ACTS prayer." The ACTS prayer is an acronym, which means each letter stands for a word:

A Adoration, which means to praise God.
C Confession, which means to tell God about your sins and ask Him to forgive you.
T Thanksgiving, which means to tell God why you are thankful for all that He has done for you.
S Supplication, which means to make a request to God.

A prayer that includes these four elements would sound like this: Dear God, I praise You for Your goodness and ask You to forgive me when I don't listen to others like I should. Thank You for my family and friends. Please be with me tomorrow when I take my math test. In Jesus's name, Amen.

2. Write the sentence in the above prayer that goes with the word below:

Adoration:

Confession:

Thanksgiving:

Supplication:

3. Now write your own ACTS prayer in the space below.

RAVENOUS PRAYER

Don't worry about anything.
Instead, tell God about everything.
Ask and pray. Give thanks to him.

(Philippians 4:6)

DAY FOUR: REAL OBEDIENCE

MAIN IDEA

It takes real obedience for us to obey God and follow His commands!

BIBLE STORY

The Parable of the Two Sons (Matthew 21:28–32).

SI'S LITTLE-KNOWN FACTS
FOR OLDER CHILDREN

- A "vineyard" is a place where grape-bearing vines are grown. The grapes are used mainly for making wines, but they are also used as table grapes, raisins, and non-alcoholic grape juice.
- The study of growing grapes is known as "viniculture."
- In the Parable of the Two Sons, we don't know which of the sons was the oldest and which was the youngest, but it doesn't matter in this story.
- To "obey" comes from the Latin word *obedire,* which means to be subject to or serve or to pay attention to.
- One of the Greek words for "obedience" gives the definition of being under someone's authority. Another Greek word for "obey" used in the New Testament means "to trust."
- True Christian obedience is not about following a rule for no reason; it's about loving someone so much that you want to follow the rules.

SI'S LITTLE-KNOWN FACTS
FOR YOUNGER CHILDREN

- A vineyard is the name of the garden used to grow grapes. Grapes are used to make grape juice and wine.
- The word "obey" comes from a word from the Latin language. Latin is another language like Spanish. The Latin word is *obedire.* It's a lot like "obey," and it means to serve or pay attention to someone.
- When we obey, it should be because we love someone and we want to make that person happy. When you love your parents, you want to please them and make them happy, so you obey them.

WORD SEARCH ANSWER KEY
(FOR OLDER CHILDREN)

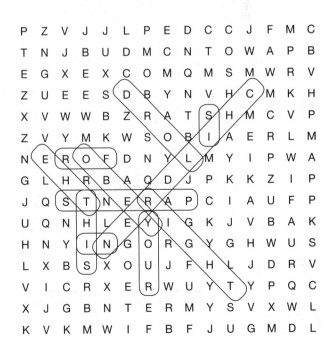

OBEDIENCE SCRIPTURE SEARCH

Obedience is important to God. In fact, throughout the Bible we find God commanding us to obey. Look up the following verses and write them on the lines provided.

Obey your parents — **Ephesians 6:1:**

_____

_____

_____

_____

Obey your teachers and leaders — **Hebrews 13:17:**

_____

_____

_____

_____

Obey your government — **Romans 13:1:**

_____

_____

_____

_____

OBEDIENCE SCRIPTURE SEARCH

Find and circle the following words in the word-search puzzle below (they are hidden horizontally, vertically, and diagonally):

CHILDREN	OBEY	YOUR
PARENTS	IN	THE
LORD	FOR	THIS
IS	RIGHT	

```
P  Z  V  J  J  L  P  E  D  C  C  J  F  M  C
T  N  J  B  U  D  M  C  N  T  O  W  A  P  B
E  G  X  E  X  C  O  M  Q  M  S  M  W  R  V
Z  U  E  E  S  D  B  Y  N  V  H  C  M  K  H
X  V  W  W  B  Z  R  A  T  S  H  M  C  V  P
Z  V  Y  M  K  W  S  O  B  I  A  E  R  L  M
N  E  R  O  F  D  N  Y  L  M  Y  I  P  W  A
G  L  H  R  B  A  Q  D  J  P  K  K  Z  I  P
J  Q  S  T  N  E  R  A  P  C  I  A  U  F  P
U  Q  N  H  L  E  Y  I  G  K  J  V  B  A  K
H  N  Y  I  N  G  O  R  G  Y  G  H  W  U  S
L  X  B  S  X  O  U  J  F  H  L  J  D  R  V
V  I  C  R  X  E  R  W  U  Y  T  Y  P  Q  C
X  J  G  B  N  T  E  R  M  Y  S  V  X  W  L
K  V  K  M  W  I  F  B  F  J  U  G  M  D  L
```

*The way we show our love
is to obey God's commands.*

2 John 1:6

DAY FIVE: ROWDY KINDNESS

MAIN IDEA

God wants us to be loud and rowdy when it comes to being kind to others!

BIBLE STORY

The Parable of the Good Samaritan (Luke 10:25–37).

SI'S LITTLE-KNOWN FACTS
FOR OLDER CHILDREN

- The road from Jerusalem to Jericho is 18 miles long and descends about 3,500 feet. After about two miles, travelers would come to a village named Bethany, at which point the road became rough. There were many rocky caves for bad men to hide out and perhaps rob someone walking by. This area was called the "bloody way." It looks the same today as it did in Jesus's day.
- The Samaritans were people of Jewish blood who had intermarried with people from other cultures. Because of this, the Jews considered them inferior. It was unheard of at the time for a Samaritan and a Jew to do things together.
- Adding to the problem was the fact that the Samaritans mixed worship of the one true God with worship of the foreign gods they had picked up.
- The word "Samaritan" was considered a bad word in Jesus's day. Today we use the word "Samaritan" to mean anyone who helps another person. God turned what was bad into something good.
- A shilling, or denarius, was worth about 17 cents. It represented the price of a day's labor.
- The word "compassion" used in this parable comes from the Greek word *splagchnizomai*, which literally means "to be moved as to one's innards." A person's innards represent the warm and tender emotions they have when they help a neighbor, friend, or someone they don't even know.

SI'S LITTLE-KNOWN FACTS
FOR YOUNGER CHILDREN

- In the Parable of the Good Samaritan, the Samaritan man was traveling from Jerusalem to Jericho. That is about 18 miles. In our car, it would only take about 20 minutes, but they did not have cars in Bible times. They had to walk.
- It was very dangerous to walk on this road because bad people would hide in caves and wait to rob the travelers.
- The Samaritans and the Jews didn't get along. So it is a surprise in this story that a Samaritan would have helped a Jewish man.
- A shilling was a type of money used in Bible times. One shilling was worth about 17 cents. It was about what someone would make for a day's work!
- The Samaritan man was "compassionate" to the man who was robbed. "Compassionate" means to do something kind for someone else because you want to help him or her.

KINDNESS MAKES A DIFFERENCE

INSTRUCTIONS: Work with another person on the following exercise. Read Luke 10:25–37 in the Bible and fill in the blanks. When you are finished, take turns reading the sentences out loud.

1. Just then a religion _____ stood up with a question to _____ Jesus. "Teacher, what do I need to do to get _____ life?"

2. He answered, "What's written in God's _____? How do you _____ it?"

3. He said, "That you _____ the Lord your God with all your _____ and _____ and _____ and _____ —and that you _____ your _____ as well as you do yourself."

4. "Good _____!" said Jesus. "Do it and you'll _____."

5. Looking for a _____, he asked, "And just how would you define '_____'?"

6. Jesus answered by telling a _____.

7. "There was once a _____ traveling from Jerusalem to _____.

8. "On the way he was attacked by _____. They took his _____, beat him up, and went off leaving him _____.

9. "Luckily, a _____ was on his way down the same _____, but when he saw him he _____ across to the other side.

10. "Then a _____ religious man showed up; he also _____ the injured man.

11. "A _____ traveling the road came on him. When he saw the man's _____, his _____ went out to him.

KINDNESS MAKES A DIFFERENCE

12. "He gave him _____ _____, disinfecting and bandaging his _____. Then he lifted

   him onto his _____, led him to an _____, and made him comfortable.

13. "In the morning he took out two silver _____ and gave them to the _____, saying,

   'Take good _____ of him. If it costs any more, put it on my _____—I'll _____

   you on my way back.'

14. "What do you think? Which of the three became a _____ to the man attacked by

   _____?"

15. "The one who treated him _____," the religion _____ responded.

16. Jesus said, "Go and do the _____."

What does the word "test" mean?

What's another word for "interpret"?

Is it easy to love your neighbor like you love yourself? Why or why not?

Why do you think Jesus used a story to tell His message?

KINDNESS

RODEO RESOURCES

BUDGET FORM

2014 BUDGETING FORM FOR WILLIE'S REDNECK RODEO

	2013 ACTUALS	2014 ESTIMATE	2014 ACTUALS
Preschool Curriculum			
Elementary Curriculum			
Opening and Closing Roundups			
Set Decorations			
Tech Supplies			
Stations			
Missy's Music and Memory			
Korie's Craft Shed			
The Warehouse			
Miss Kay's Kitchen			
Si's Bull Pen			
Promotion/Event Cost			
Advertisements			
Pre-event Mailing			
Post-event Mailing (follow-up)			
T-shirts			
Site decorations			
Volunteers			
VBS Volunteer Meeting Food/Meals			
Volunteer T-shirts			
Other			
TOTAL EXPENSES			

CHECK-IN/CHECK-OUT SHEET

Group Name: _____ Date: _____

LAST NAME	FIRST NAME	AGE	SIGN IN (INITIAL)	TIME	SIGN OUT (INITIAL)	TIME

NOTE: Have preapproved parents or guardians initial the box at check-in and again at check-out.

VOLUNTEER FORM

CONTACT INFORMATION

Last Name: _____ First Name: _____ Middle Initial: _____

Address: _____

Phone Number: _____ Email address: _____

REFERENCES

Who are three people who would know about your qualifications to serve?

Name: _____

Phone Number: _____ Email address: _____

Name: _____

Phone Number: _____ Email address: _____

Name: _____

Phone Number: _____ Email address: _____

PERSONAL INFORMATION

Have you ever been convicted of a felony?

❑ Yes

❑ No

Why do you want to volunteer in children's ministry?

What are your main areas of giftedness (see 1 Corinthians 12; Romans 12)?

Which of the following would you most enjoy at the VBS (check up to four)?

- ❑ Administration/registration/assisting the VBS director
- ❑ Contacting/recruiting volunteers
- ❑ Performing in short skits
- ❑ Singing/performing in a band
- ❑ Leading/helping lead the song and Scripture memory time
- ❑ Leading/helping lead the craft time
- ❑ Leading/helping lead games
- ❑ Leading/helping lead the snack time
- ❑ Leading/helping lead fun facts and activities time

What experiences do you have in working with children?

What age groups do you prefer working with?

FOR INTERNAL USE ONLY:

Interview Completed: ❑ Yes ❑ No

Date: _____ By: _____

State license screening/criminal check completed: ❑ Yes ❑ No

Date: _____ By: _____

REGISTRATION FORM

Last Name: _____ First Name: _____ Middle Initial: _____

Grade in Fall: _____ Age: _____

Name of friends attending VBS:

Please list any special needs or physical limitations:

Please list any food allergies:

Will you be purchasing a T-Shirt? ❑ Yes ❑ No

If yes, what is the T-Shirt size? ❑ XS ❑ S ❑ M ❑ L ❑ XL

Is there anything else we should know?

Please list the name of the individual who is authorized to check out the child:

Last Name: _____ First Name: _____ Middle Initial: _____

Cell Phone: _____ Email address: _____

Address: _____

Who should we contact in case of emergency?

Last Name: _____ First Name: _____ Middle Initial: _____

Cell Phone: _____ Email address: _____

Note: Individuals authorized to pick up the child will need to show a valid photo ID at the time of check out. Your child will not be released without proper identification. Thank you for your cooperation.

[Optional: Include any payment information here, such as the cost of the VBS, to whom the parent/ guardian should send the payment, the form of payment that can be accepted, and so forth.]

PARENT LETTER

NOTE: Parents and/or guardians should receive this letter after registering their children for Willie's Redneck Rodeo VBS. As an option, insert the Willie's Redneck Rodeo logo on the letter (see the DVD-ROM for a JPEG of the logo).

Welcome to Willie's Redneck Rodeo!

We're so glad that you'll be joining us and the Robertson family from *Duck Dynasty*® on *[insert VBS dates and times]* for the greatest rodeo of all time!

Rodeos are filled with cowboys falling off bulls, horses knocking down barrels, and colorful clowns keeping everyone laughing. There's something for everyone! In truth, life is kind of like a rodeo. It's filled with falling down, getting back up, brushing yourself off, and trying again. It's also full of clowning around! God has created a mighty entertaining world in which we can learn to love Him and the people around us.

Willie, Korie, Phil, Miss Kay, Jase, Jep, and the whole Robertson gang all love the parables that Jesus told in the Bible. Christ was a powerful storyteller, and He knew how to get to the heart and mind of a person with the stories He told! *Willie's Redneck Rodeo* is filled with these stories of Jesus—as told through the modern-day exploits of the Robertson family. Each day, your children will have the opportunity to learn more about these stories of Jesus through music, games, arts and crafts, activities, and more!

So y'all need to put on those cowboy hats and start practicing those southern accents, because it's time for *Willie's Redneck Rodeo*! We'll be praying that your children will have fun during their time at VBS, but even more importantly, that they will grow in their faith as they learn more about God.

In Him,

[insert director's signature]